A TASTE OF CHINATOWN

A Saturday afternoon in Chinatown, jam-packed with shoppers and restaurant-goers.

A TASTE OF

CHINATOWN

AMERICA'S NATIVE CHINESE CUISINE

JOIE WARNER

DESIGNED AND PHOTOGRAPHED
BY DREW WARNER

CROWN PUBLISHERS, INC., NEW YORK

Published by Crown Publishers, Inc.,
201 East 50th Street
New York, New York 10022
Member of the Crown Publishing Group.

CROWN is a trademark of Crown Publishers, Inc.
Manufactured in the United States of America

Book Design and Photographs:
Drew Warner
Food Styling, Props, and Set Design:
Drew and Joie Warner
Color Separations:
Colour Technologies
Typesetting:
Cybergraphics

LIBRARY OF CONGRESS
CATALOGING-IN-PUBLICATION DATA
Warner, Joie.
        A taste of Chinatown: America's native
Chinese cuisine / Joie Warner ; designed
and photographed by Drew Warner.
        p.   cm.
"A Flavor book" — T.p. verso.
Includes index.
1.Cookery, Chinese.   I. Warner, Drew.
II. Title.
TX724.5.C5W37 1991
641.5951 — dc20   90-22275
                                                CIP
ISBN 0-517-58408-5

This book was created and produced by
Flavor Publications, Inc.
208 East 51st Street, Suite 240
New York, New York 10022

10 9 8 7 6 5 4 3 2 1

FIRST AMERICAN EDITION

DEDICATED to the people of Chinatown.

Acknowledgments

A very special thanks to Erica Marcus
and to everyone at Crown Publishers for
their enthusiasm for our book.
Thanks to my friend Frances Hanna for
her keen eye (especially on all those
hyphens!) and her editorial expertise.
And to my friend Ella Yoa, a Chinese
cooking teacher and excellent cook, for
sharing with me the versatile marinade
formula I've used in a few of my own
recipes, as well as coming into my
kitchen to cook and share her
techniques.

.   .   .   .

IF *you want your dinner nicely cooked.*
Don't offend the cook.

—CHINESE PROVERB

A typical Chinatown eatery where decor is secondary to the food.

CONTENTS

CHINATOWN A TOWN WITHIN A CITY

The flavor of China—and its sights, smells, and sounds—transported to America.

For me, visiting any Chinatown is an exotic adventure, like being in a different country. Walking along the streets — looking at their signs in Chinese, hearing musical Cantonese conversations around me, seeing countless Chinese shoppers and street hawkers — makes me feel as if I'm in the Orient, even if I'm only a few blocks from my own neighborhood. I've shopped in my local Chinatown weekly over the years, but still marvel at what an intriguing place it is. To explore Chinatown is to discover culinary delights at the numerous eateries that it packs together block after block. And once you discover the ways of the wok, Chinatown becomes a food shopping district, too. For some, it's a tourist attraction; for others, a bargain hunter's or a collector's delight: the place to find lacquerware, bamboo furniture, gifts ranging from priceless jade to bright paper lanterns, and all things Chinese. ■ For the Chinese, Chinatown is a necessity — a self-contained community with Hong Kong banks and Chinese movie theaters and pharmacies, Chinese lawyers, doctors, accountants, and others providing essential services. There are Chinese newspapers, record, book, and music stores, benevolent societies, and clothing stores. It's a home away from home for immigrant Chinese — a refuge in a strange country. For these newcomers and to second- third- and fourth-generation Chinese-Americans alike, Chinatown is their social haven for tea, lunch, dinner, and family celebrations. And during the biggest annual celebration of all — the Chinese New Year festivities — the area explodes with activity. ■ Chinatown is a lively neighborhood always crowded with people — a neighborhood that thrives on street life from morning to late at night, especially on weekends when it's jam-packed with Chinese of all ages who come to shop, meet friends, go to the movies, and eat. The streets are thronged with people laden with their purchases from shops full of extraordinary produce that often spills right out onto the sidewalks. ■ Chinatown's food shops display Oriental vegetables, fruit — and other goods that seem strange to Western eyes — unceremoniously in the cardboard or wooden boxes they were shipped in. Sidewalk browsers poke through fragrant ginger, crisp bok choy, fresh water chestnuts, gnarled mustard greens, pungent coriander, flowering chives, and baskets of bean sprouts. ■ Inside the shops there is a bewildering array of unusual canned goods: loquats, litchis, bamboo shoots, straw mushrooms, and pickled cabbage to name a very few.

Packages of dried items such as tangerine peels, oysters, shrimps, bird's nest, shark's fin, tree ears, black mushrooms, lily buds, and oodles of dried noodles crowd the shelves. Bottles and huge restaurant-size cans of soy sauce, hoisin sauce, plum sauce, oyster sauce, bean sauce, sesame oil, and chili oil pack even more shelves. The refrigerators are stocked with pails of bean curd, packages of Chinese sausage, wrappers for won tons, spring rolls, and a cornucopia of fresh noodles in myriad varieties. The freezers contain boxes of shrimp in assorted sizes, along with frozen squid, crab, abalone, fish balls, and crab claws. Many of the food shops have fish counters selling fresh seafood. Meat counters display fresh standard fare as well as all sorts of odds and ends that are unfamiliar to Westerners. Some shops have tanks filled with live carp, lobsters — even turtles ready for cleaning. ■ Along the streets, barbecue-shop windows tempt passersby with glistening roast ducks, chickens, and spareribs displayed on hooks. Once inside these Chinese delis, it's astonishing to see the choice of prepared ready-to-serve goodies: Chinese barbecued pork (char siu); whole roasted pigs; roast duck and chicken; gizzards and livers, chicken wings and feet; bright orange cuttlefish, and other tempting staples. Glazed with each shop's secret hoisin-based sauces, these items are cooked (by baking in special ovens, not barbecuing in the true sense of the word), then made ready to be custom chopped into bite-sized pieces for the purchaser. The Chinese use these delicacies as snacks or side dishes, or add them to soups and stir-fries. ■ There are Chinese bakeries selling buns and pastries filled with sweetened bean paste, also almond cookies, sponge cakes, moon cakes, custard-filled tarts, and a broad assortment of ready-to-heat dim sum specialties such as char siu bow (barbecued pork buns) and spring rolls. And every Chinatown has its hardware and gift shops specializing in Oriental cookware. ■ We in America are fortunate to have the most vibrant and populated non-native Chinatowns in the world. New York's Chinatown is reputed to have the largest Chinese population in America, with over 350,000 Chinese — and in San Francisco, our second largest community, the Chinese account for over 200,000. ■ America has smaller Chinatowns or Chinese communities in Los Angeles, Boston, Washington, and Chicago, plus Chinese-Americans scattered throughout most smaller cities and towns. ■ Over the past 20 years, New York's Chinatown population has multiplied eight times, blurring the lines between Chinatown and neighboring Little Italy. With its more than 200 restaurants — ranging from humble noodle houses to extravagant branches of Hong Kong establishments — New York's Chinatown has become a gastronomic paradise. San Francisco's Chinatown is equally notable for its excellent Chinese food, particularly its

Joie lights the candles before seating her guests.

seafood dishes. It's also America's *oldest* and most famous Chinatown. ■ Visitors from Hong Kong and recent immigrants alike confirm that Chinatowns across America offer some of the finest, most authentic Chinese cuisine outside Asia. Noted food and travel writers have remarked that when visiting our Chinatowns it's difficult to remember they're in America. ■ It's been over 20 years since I first set foot in my local Chinatown, but from that moment I became captivated with — then addicted to — Chinese food. At that time there were only a few restaurants serving mostly Cantonese or pseudo-Chinese fare such as egg rolls, chop suey, and sweet and sour bo bo balls. This was partly because of the difficulty in obtaining authentic ingredients and partly to attract non-Chinese customers in order to stay in business at a time when the Chinese community was still quite small. Today Chinatown restaurants have expanded to include the four major culinary regions of China: Cantonese — subtle, fresh cooking; Szechuan and Hunan — much of it hot and spicy; Peking — full-flavored, often referred to as Mandarin cooking; and Shanghai — considered the most sophisticated cuisine in China because it has borrowed techniques and ingredients from the other three regions. ■ Over the years, Drew and I have explored many Chinatowns right across America, always in search of the most authentic restaurants serving the best won ton soup, the crispiest spring rolls, the hottest Kung Pao Chicken, the most delicate dim sum! Along the way, I started trying to recreate the tastes of Chinatown in my own kitchen. At first I tried persuading my favorite restaurants to share a recipe or two with me, but soon discovered that no Chinese chef worth his soy sauce ever uses recipes — they cook by instinct and experience instead! Besides, most restaurateurs wrongly believe that if they give away a recipe you'll never return to eat there! A few chefs did let me spend some time in their kitchens, but most of my recipes are the result of visiting a restaurant several times to eat, taste, carefully analyze the ingredients, take notes, and then go home to my own kitchen to test my theories. In the end, I've created recipes that can't really be credited to any particular restaurant though they're close facsimiles of my own favorite Chinatown dishes. ■ The recipes in this book are not for the type of innovative East-meets-West dishes that some of today's chefs are experimenting with; rather they're for many of the exciting, yet familiar dishes that Chinese food lovers have taken delight in when eating out in Chinatown. This book is designed to help you create these dishes in your own kitchen as authentically as possible. Part of the fun and pleasure of eating Chinese-style is that several dishes are served at the same time and shared by all. The general rule is to serve one dish for each person at the meal, e.g., four dishes (plus rice) for four persons, six dishes for six persons. I have made a few serving suggestions, but mostly you should mix and match dishes that appeal to you, keeping in mind the Chinese principle of always planning a meal around complementary flavors, textures, and colors: salty or sour and sweet; hot and mild; subtle and pungent; tender and crunchy. And never serve a selection of dishes that have all been cooked the same way, or dishes with sauces all of the same color. Serve instead one stir-fried dish (or two if you're experienced with stir-frying), a deep-fried dish, a soup, a cold dish, a braised dish or one that can be prepared ahead of time and reheated. ■ I've had fun discovering the tastes of Chinatown. Even if you've yet to visit a Chinatown, I hope the recipes in this book will inspire you not only to venture there, but also to recreate some of its flavors in your own kitchen.

JOIE WARNER

Tiered bamboo steamers contain the Chinese delicacies and snacks known as dim sum.

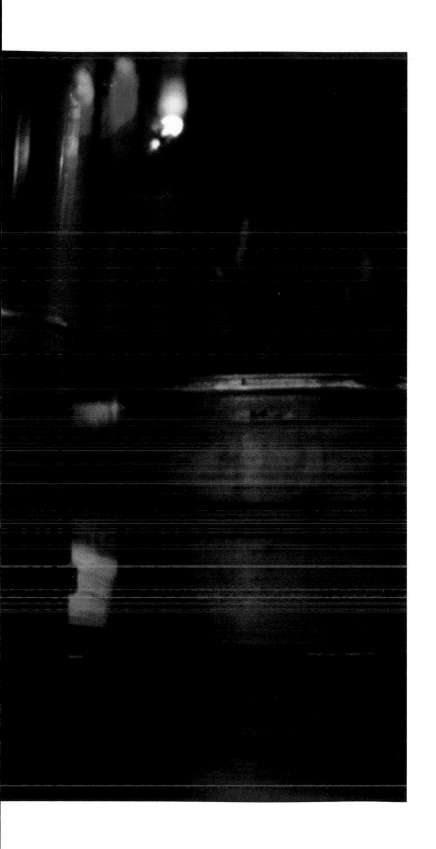

APPETIZERS

Crispy spring rolls served with a selection of dips: Chinese chili sauce, Worcestershire sauce, Chinese mustard, and plum sauce.

SHRIMP-STUFFED SPRING ROLLS

O ne of the most popular of all Cantonese snacks, these crispy treats are wrapped with paper-thin spring roll skins (not egg roll wrappers) and stuffed with shrimp and barely-fried vegetables. Most Americans serve plum sauce or mustard with spring rolls, but I prefer a few dashes of Worcestershire sauce as do many Chinese – that's why you'll find it on tables in restaurants throughout Chinatown. Deep-frying at the temperature specified in the recipe and never overcrowding the frying vessel is the secret to non-oily spring rolls. They are best when fried and served immediately, but you can fry the rolls ahead of time, then reheat by placing them on a rack set on a baking sheet, and baking in a 450°F oven for 7 minutes or until crisp.

3 tablespoons vegetable oil
2 large garlic cloves, finely chopped
2 tablespoons finely chopped fresh ginger
½ pound raw shrimp, peeled and diced
½ pound Chinese barbecued pork, shredded
10 Chinese dried black mushrooms, stems snapped off, caps soaked for 30 minutes in hot water, squeezed dry and diced
6 large whole green onions, finely chopped
1 large celery stalk, finely chopped
1 large carrot, cut into fine julienne
1 pound (about 8 cups) bean sprouts (not washed)

SEASONING LIQUID
Combine in bowl:
1 tablespoon soy sauce
2 teaspoons sesame oil
1 teaspoon salt

(seasoning liquid continued)
1 teaspoon sugar
½ teaspoon five spice powder
2 teaspoons potato or cornstarch

13 ounce (369 g) package spring roll skins (round type best), thawed in package, but do not open package
1 egg, lightly beaten
3 cups oil for deep-frying
Worcestershire sauce for dipping
Plum sauce for dipping

MUSTARD DIPPING SAUCE
Combine in small dish:
1 tablespoon Dijon mustard
1 teaspoon sesame oil

. . . .

1. Heat wok on high heat. Add oil; when hot, add garlic and ginger. Cook a few seconds; add shrimp. Toss for 30 seconds; add pork and

vegetables except bean sprouts. Stir-fry for 2 minutes or until vegetables are crisp-tender. Add bean sprouts; toss for 1 minute – no longer.

2. Restir *seasoning liquid.* Pour into wok; toss until combined. Immediately remove to a large baking sheet, spreading out mixture so it will cool quickly. Allow to cool completely to room temperature before using.

3. Before removing spring roll skins from package, grasp package with both hands and flex repeatedly, turning package at the same time, to loosen skins from each other. Remove them from package. Peel back one skin about 1 inch all the way around, then gently peel off. Repeat and stack remaining skins. Cover with a damp cloth to prevent them from drying out.

4. Put about 2 tablespoons cooled filling in center of the lower half of skin; fold over from the bottom fairly tightly to cover filling. Then roll it to the center. Fold the two sides toward center; moisten the sides and top flap generously with beaten egg (I do this with my fingers) and continue rolling to form a cylinder. Make sure each

roll is completely sealed or oil will seep in while frying. Set aside, seam side down. Repeat until all are done. Do not allow spring rolls to remain uncooked for more than an hour, or filling may soak through skins.

5. Heat wok on high heat. Add oil; heat to 375°F. Lower 4 to 6 spring rolls into oil; cook for about 2 to 3 minutes or until golden brown, turning occasionally. Remove to a paper towel-lined plate to drain. Bring oil temperature back to 375°F before adding next batch; continue

until all are done.

6. Serve immediately with a choice of Worcestershire sauce, plum sauce, and Mustard Dipping Sauce.

Makes about 24 rolls.

POT STICKERS

P ork-stuffed dumplings are first fried, then steam-cooked, and fried again to produce dumplings that are delightfully crunchy on the bottom yet soft and tender at the top. Legend has it these pan-fried dumplings were created by mistake when a cook at the Imperial Palace was preparing boiled dumplings. He walked away from the stove and totally forgot about them (I've done that a few times myself!). When he returned, the water had evaporated and they were browned and crusty on the bottom. He nervously served them to the royal family and, luckily for him and the rest of us, the Emperor was pleased with the results. The dumplings are time-consuming to prepare if you make your own wrappers (you can purchase ready-made dumpling wrappers in Chinatown food shops in the fresh noodle section) but happily, the dough and dumplings can be made ahead and either refrigerated or frozen before pan-frying and steaming. Once cooked, they can be left in the pan for up to an hour before serving time, then gently reheated, adding a little more oil if necessary. Or to reheat the next day, bring them to room temperature, place in a nonstick pan with about 1 tablespoon water, cover, and steam-cook on medium heat for 5 minutes or until heated through and crisp on the bottom.

2 cups finely chopped Chinese
cabbage
1 teaspoon salt
¾ pound ground pork

SEASONINGS
½ cup chopped whole green onions
⅓ cup chopped fresh coriander
leaves (optional)
2 large garlic cloves, finely chopped
1 tablespoon finely chopped fresh
ginger
Grated zest of 1 medium orange
2 tablespoons soy sauce
2 tablespoons sesame oil
1 tablespoon dry sherry
1 tablespoon potato or cornstarch

1 package dumpling wrappers *or*

DUMPLING WRAPPERS
2 cups all-purpose flour
1 cup boiling water

Vegetable oil for frying
¾ cup chicken stock
Worcestershire sauce for dipping

1. Toss chopped cabbage and salt in mixing bowl. Let stand 5 minutes. Take handfuls of cabbage; squeeze out excess liquid and place in clean large bowl. Add ground pork and *seasonings;* combine well (hands work best). Cover and refrigerate until ready to use.

2. If not using ready-made dumpling wrappers, place flour in food processor; add boiling water while machine is running and continue until dough forms a ball. Remove dough, knead for 30 seconds, and cover with plastic wrap. Let rest 20 minutes.

3. Roll into a cylinder about 18 inches long and 1 inch in diameter. Cut in half; cut each half into 25 pieces. Press each piece down with palm of hand to flatten slightly. Using rolling pin, roll each disk, between two pieces of plastic wrap, into a 4-inch circle. Don't stack or they will stick together. Keep circles covered with a damp cloth to prevent drying out.

4. Spoon about 1 tablespoon filling into center of each dumpling wrapper. If using packaged dumpling wrappers, brush edges lightly with water to help seal — not necessary with freshly-made. Fold over to make a half circle.

5. With your fingers, make about 6 pleats across dumpling, pinching to

seal. It should curve into an arc shape on the top and be flat on the bottom. Set completed dumplings on a lightly cornstarched baking sheet. May be refrigerated several hours, covered, or frozen. Partially thaw before pan-frying.

6. Heat a 12-inch nonstick skillet over medium-high heat. Add 3 tablespoons oil; when hot, place pot stickers, flat side down, in concentric circles, each dumpling touching the next. (They should all fit in skillet; otherwise do 2 batches.) Tilt and gently shake pan to distribute oil evenly. Fry for 2 to 3 minutes or until bottoms are golden brown, checking frequently. Be careful not to brown too much.

7. Pour in chicken stock, cover, gently boil over medium heat for about 10 minutes or until stock evaporates. When you hear a sizzling sound, drizzle in 1 tablespoon oil, tilting skillet to distribute oil underneath dumplings. Fry for about 5 minutes or until bottoms are crisp and golden brown. Use a spatula to loosen bottoms of pot stickers, if necessary. Carefully invert onto a serving plate or platter, browned side up.

Serve with Worcestershire sauce.

Makes about 50 dumplings.

BRAISED CHINESE MUSHROOMS

W oodsy and aromatic, Chinese dried mushrooms become even more lusty and intensely flavored when simmered in a garlic and soy braising liquid. They are wonderful served cold or at room temperature — though it's difficult not to indulge in a few mushrooms hot from the pot! Dried mushrooms vary in both quality and price. The best are floral mushrooms which are quite large and meaty with white cracks on the surface. The lesser grade, medium-size dried mushrooms are used mainly for everyday cooking, but if you want to use them for this dish, then double the quantity. It's important to rinse the mushrooms well, both before and after soaking, otherwise sand will seep into the soaking liquid and be reabsorbed while braising. Serve these gorgeous, dark, glistening mushrooms as part of an appetizer plate or as a separate dish with the main course.

12 large Chinese dried black mushrooms, about 2½ to 3 inches in diameter (or 24 medium-size)

SEASONING LIQUID
2 tablespoons sugar
2 tablespoons soy sauce
1 tablespoon vegetable oil
1 tablespoon sesame oil
½ teaspoon salt
4 large garlic cloves, peeled and left whole
4 quarter-size slices fresh ginger

1 tablespoon oyster sauce

1. Snap off mushroom stems; rinse caps well under cold running water to remove any sand. Soak caps in 1½ cups hot water for 30 minutes or until softened. Place a strainer in bowl; line strainer with a paper towel to trap sand and drain mushrooms, reserving liquid. (It's best to rinse mushrooms again under running water to remove any remaining sand.)

2. Bring mushroom liquid and *seasoning liquid,* including garlic and ginger, to a boil in heavy, medium saucepan. Add mushrooms; bring back to a boil, then reduce heat to medium-low. Simmer mushrooms, stirring occasionally, for about 45 minutes or until just a *very* thin film of liquid remains. A little moisture is

necessary to mix with the oyster sauce.

3. Turn off heat, add oyster sauce to mushrooms, and stir until they are evenly coated. Serve immediately, at room temperature, or chilled.

Makes 12 large or 24 medium mushrooms.

Mushroom caps braised in a pungent broth are a time-honored delicacy at Chinese banquets.

Place a dish of these delightful pecans on the bar and see how long they last!

SUGARED PECANS OR WALNUTS

The first time we attended a Chinese banquet we were delighted —if a little surprised — to experience these sweet "appetite teasers" served along with pickled vegetables and cold seafood and meats. Of course, we really shouldn't have been because, as everyone knows, the Chinese love to combine contrasting flavors and textures — sweet, sour, hot, cold, soft, and crunchy. These nuts are first boiled to remove any bitterness, lightly cooked in a sugar syrup, tossed again with sugar, and deep-fried until mahogany-colored. Candied pecans — and their walnut cousins — are just sweet enough and so irresistibly crunchy as to be addictive. They are a terrific accompaniment to champagne or cocktails.

4 cups water
12 ounces (about 2½ cups) pecan or
   walnut halves

GLAZE
⅓ cup sugar
¼ cup water

¼ cup sugar
2 cups oil for deep-frying

1. Bring 4 cups water to a boil in heavy saucepan. Add pecans, reduce heat, and simmer for 5 minutes to remove bitterness. Drain well in a sieve, discarding water.

2. In same saucepan, add *glaze*; bring to a boil on medium heat. Boil for 1 minute without stirring.

3. Add pecans; stir constantly for 2 to 3 minutes with rubber spatula or until they are coated with glaze and all liquid has evaporated. Immediately remove saucepan from heat; add ¼ cup sugar and toss until nuts are evenly coated with sugar.

4. Remove pecans to 2 large pieces of wax paper large enough that they can be spread out to dry without clumping. Gently separate any nuts that are attached to each other.

5. Heat wok on high heat. Add oil; heat to 350°F. Deep-fry pecans in 3 batches, reheating oil between batches, stirring constantly for about 2 minutes each time or until they are caramelized and golden brown. Be careful not to burn. Drain on another large piece of wax paper. Separate nuts, cool, and store in an airtight container for up to a week (if they last that long!).

Serves 8.

SHRIMP TOAST

T hese are delightful with drinks before dinner, although I often make a meal of them, plus one or two other appetizers, with soup or green tea. Shrimp toast are also superb as part of a main course. Be sure to dry out the bread sufficiently before frying, so that very little oil will be absorbed. If you are in a hurry and don't have the time to dry them overnight, you can place slices in a 250° F oven for 10 minutes or so. You may substitute regular white bread and cut it into a variety of shapes — triangles, rounds, etc. — but the taste and texture of the toasts will not be quite the same. Shrimp toast are best when deep-fried and served at once. You may prepare them several hours ahead and then deep-fry just before serving. It's fun to create different designs with the sesame-seed toppings, they're not only dramatic-looking, they taste terrific, too! Don't leave out the coriander ones, though. To coriander lovers, they're absolutely wonderful!

1 large whole green onion, coarsely chopped
1 tablespoon coarsely chopped fresh ginger
1 pound raw shrimp, peeled and deveined
1 egg
1 teaspoon dry sherry
1 teaspoon soy sauce
2 teaspoons sesame oil
½ teaspoon salt
White sesame seeds (garnish)
Black sesame seeds (garnish)
Fresh coriander leaves (garnish)
2 to 3 French baguettes, about 2 inches in diameter, (to yield 40 slices) sliced about ¼ inch thick, and allowed to dry out overnight
Oil for deep-frying

1. Chop green onion and ginger in food processor. Add shrimp; process to a paste. Add egg, sherry, soy sauce, sesame oil, and salt. Combine.

2. Place sesame seeds on separate plates. Choose the largest and freshest coriander leaves – 3 to a sprig is prettiest – and set aside.

3. Spread each piece of bread with about 1 tablespoon of shrimp paste, mounding slightly in center. Press it down gently so that it doesn't fall off bread when frying.

4. Garnish the bread slices using the following methods: lightly dip the top of a few slices in a little of the black sesame seeds to cover the center, then dip edges in white seeds to finish, or vice versa. Now dip some of the slices completely in white seeds and a few completely in black. Or make even halves of black and white. Another variation, without seeds, is to place a sprig of coriander in the center of some slices. The finished slices may be done ahead to this point, loosely covered, and refrigerated for several hours before frying. Bring back to room temperature before frying.

5. Heat wok on high heat. Add 2 cups oil; heat to 350° F. Deep-fry a few toasts at a time, shrimp side down, for 30 seconds or until golden brown. Turn over; fry for another 30 seconds or until lightly browned. Do not overcook. Remove with tongs or slotted strainer to a paper towel-lined plate to drain. Serve at once.

Makes about 40 shrimp toast.

A spectacular starter, shrimp toast are so good that there are never enough.

SWEET AND SPICY CUCUMBER SALAD

I especially like to serve this refreshing salad as part of a multicourse Chinese meal, or serve it in the traditional way as a cold appetizer along with other cold dishes such as Braised Mushrooms (page 20). Make this salad just prior to serving to retain crispness and flavor.

1 large English cucumber, unpeeled
  and cut into thin slices
1 teaspoon salt
2 tablespoons vegetable oil
2 large garlic cloves, finely chopped
1 teaspoon crushed Szechuan
  peppercorns

SEASONING LIQUID
Combine in bowl:
3 tablespoons sesame oil
2 tablespoons rice vinegar
2 teaspoons sugar
½ teaspoon hot red pepper flakes
2 tablespoons very finely shredded
  fresh ginger

Black sesame seeds (optional garnish)

1. Place cucumber slices in bowl; sprinkle with salt and toss to coat evenly. Set aside for 20 minutes. Rinse well under cold water; pat dry with paper towels. The cucumber slices must be dried well or dressing will be watery. Place in clean bowl.

2. Heat small skillet over medium heat. Add vegetable oil; when hot, add garlic and peppercorns, and cook a few seconds until fragrant. Remove from heat. Immediately pour in *seasoning liquid,* stir, and pour over cucumber slices. Mix and serve at room temperature. Transfer to a serving dish; garnish with sesame seeds if desired.

Serves 2 to 4.

MANDARIN PANCAKES OR GREEN ONION CAKES

M andarin Pancakes are served in Northern and Central China as a staple instead of rice. They are more familiar here as an accompaniment to stir-fried dishes such as Mu Shu Pork or Peking Duck. Easily done ahead, they can be fried, stacked between pieces of wax paper, then frozen. Defrost and steam for 5 minutes before serving. Green Onion Cakes are made from the same dough but with chopped green onions added. Though not traditional, you can substitute chopped fresh coriander for the green onions to make Coriander Cakes. Green Onion Cakes do not freeze well once they are cooked, but they can be stacked as described above before cooking, covered with plastic wrap, and refrigerated several hours before frying. They are splendid with hot soup or as part of a multicourse meal.

2 cups all-purpose flour
½ teaspoon salt
1 cup boiling water

Sesame oil for brushing pancakes
1 cup finely chopped green onions
  (for Green Onion Cakes only)
Oil for frying
Salt

1. In food processor, mix flour and salt. Leave running, and pour in boiling water. Stop machine as soon as mixture forms a ball. Remove and knead for 1 minute or until smooth and satiny. Wrap ball in plastic wrap; set aside 30 minutes to rest. At this point, the dough can be refrigerated for up to 2 days.

2. Place dough on a lightly floured surface; lightly flour rolling pin. Form dough into a cylinder about 18 inches long and 1 inch in diameter. Cut roll into 18 equal-size segments; roll each segment into a ball.

3. For Mandarin Pancakes: Place 3 tablespoons sesame oil in small dish. Using the palm of your hand, slightly flatten 2 of the dough balls. Brush one side of each disk generously with sesame oil. Place the two oiled surfaces together on top of each other. Repeat until all dough balls are done. Using rolling pin, roll out each double circle to form 6-inch pancakes. Heat a nonstick skillet over medium heat. Cook pancakes for 1 minute each side or until nicely speckled with brown spots. Be careful not to overcook or the pancakes will dry out — they should be supple, not brittle. Remove from pan, allow to cool a few seconds, then pull them apart and stack them on top of each other. Repeat until all are done. To steam: Place the stack of pancakes in heatproof dish on rack in steamer above boiling water. Cover; steam for 5 minutes or until soft. Remove;

fold in half or in quarters.

4. To make Green Onion Cakes: Using the palm of your hand, slightly flatten all the dough balls into disks. Using oiled rolling pin, roll disks, on a piece of plastic wrap, into 4-inch circles. Don't stack or they will stick together. Brush the tops of pancakes generously with sesame oil and sprinkle with green onions.

5. Roll each one into a cylinder jelly-roll-style; pinch edges to seal. Coil them into a circle; pinch the ends to seal. Using rolling pin, roll coils into 4-inch pancakes.

6. If not cooking immediately, stack between pieces of wax paper, cover with plastic wrap and refrigerate for several hours.

7. Heat large nonstick skillet on high heat. Add enough oil to lightly coat bottom of pan. When hot, fry a few cakes at a time, making sure the edges do not touch, for about 2 minutes each side or until golden brown, adding oil between batches. Remove from pan; sprinkle with salt and serve. May be kept warm in a 200°F oven for a few minutes before serving.

Makes about 18 pancakes.

. . . .

DELICATE SHRIMP DUMPLINGS

Wherever there is a large Chinese community, you'll find restaurants offering dim sum — the Cantonese lunchtime specialty of serving tea with sweet or savory bite-size delicacies of many kinds, be they steamed in little bamboo baskets, deep-fried, braised, or baked. The waitresses or waiters push carts around the restaurant while calling out the names of each item in Chinese: har gow (shrimp dumplings), siu mai (pork dumplings), woh tip (pot stickers), and so on. Luckily, you don't need to know the names, just be adventurous and point to whatever looks interesting — whether on the trolley or at the next table! Much as I enjoy dim sum in Chinatown, I still find it extremely rewarding to make these little morsels at home. And while mine may not look quite as perfect as a chef's, they're just as delicious. These are best prepared and served immediately, but the uncooked dumplings can be covered with plastic wrap and refrigerated for a few hours before steaming.

1 cup wheat starch
2 tablespoons potato or cornstarch
Pinch salt
1 tablespoon vegetable oil
1 cup boiling water

FILLING
½ pound raw shrimp, peeled,
   deveined, and diced
3 tablespoons coarsely diced
   bamboo shoots

SEASONINGS
2 teaspoons minced fresh ginger
½ teaspoon salt
¼ teaspoon sugar
⅛ teaspoon white pepper
1½ teaspoons potato or cornstarch
2 teaspoons sesame oil

Worcestershire sauce for dipping
Chinese chili sauce for dipping

1. In food processor, mix starches and salt. Add oil; with motor running, pour boiling water through feed tube and continue processing until dough forms a ball. Remove from food processor, then knead dough (be careful: it's hot) for 30 seconds or until smooth and satiny. Cover completely with plastic wrap; set aside. Do not refrigerate — this dough can't be made ahead.

2. Using hands or chopsticks, combine shrimp, bamboo shoots, and *seasonings* in bowl. Mix well. Set aside.

3. Divide dough into 3 parts and keep covered so that it doesn't dry out.

4. Roll out one part into a cylinder about 1 inch in diameter. Cut into pieces about ½-inch thick – not much thicker or wrapper will be doughy. Place on an oiled tortilla press (or use an oiled rolling pin to roll circles out on a 6 x 10-inch piece of plastic wrap) to roll each wrapper into a 3-inch circle — no larger. The dough must be thin. If too thick it will look and taste doughy. Cover with a damp towel and continue until all are done.

5. Hold each wrapper in palm of hand and place about 1 teaspoon filling in center — don't overstuff. Fold over to make a half circle. (The dough will crack if not handled carefully and will break open while steaming.)

6. With your fingers, make about 5 or 6 tiny pleats across dumpling, pinching to seal. It should curve into an arc shape on the top. Set completed dumplings on a lightly cornstarched baking sheet. At this point they can be refrigerated for a few hours, covered.

7. Lightly oil bottom of heatproof dish (I use a Pyrex pie plate); arrange several dumplings on it, leaving space in between each dumpling to allow steam to circulate.

8. Place a rack in wok and fill with water to bottom edge of rack. Cover; bring to a boil. Place dumplings in dish on rack over boiling water, cover, and steam for about 6 minutes or until shrimp are cooked. Do not overcook. Continue until all are done. Serve at once with Worcestershire sauce and chili sauce.

Makes about 30 dumplings.

PORK DUMPLINGS

S econd to shrimp dumplings (har gow) in popularity, siu mai (pork dumplings) translates as "cook and sell", meaning these are so appealing, they're guaranteed to sell out. Siu Mai are easier to make than Har Gow because you don't have to make the dumpling wrapper: won ton wrappers hold the stuffing in. Be sure to purchase the thinnest won ton wrappers available or they'll be tough when steamed. Regular ground pork works fine in the filling, or better yet, use ½ pound lean pork and 3 ounces pork fatback cut into 2-inch pieces, then chopped with a cleaver (not a food processor) into tiny cubes for the most authentic texture. Siu Mai can be cooked and resteamed, although there is some loss of flavor. It is best to make ahead, refrigerate several hours, and then steam just before serving. You can freeze stuffed dumplings for up to 1 month. Partially thaw before steaming.

½ pound ground pork
½ pound raw shrimp, peeled and diced
6 Chinese dried black mushrooms, stems snapped off, caps soaked for 30 minutes in hot water, squeezed dry, and diced
3 large whole green onions, finely chopped

SEASONINGS
½ teaspoon salt
½ teaspoon sugar
¼ teaspoon white pepper
1 tablespoon potato or cornstarch
4 tablespoons water
2 teaspoons sesame oil

1 package *thin* won ton wrappers
Small piece of sweet red pepper, diced
Fresh coriander leaves
Worcestershire sauce for dipping
Chinese chili sauce for dipping

1. Using hands or chopsticks, mix pork, shrimp, mushrooms, green onions, and *seasonings* in large bowl.

2. Scoop up mixture, then throw it against the inside of the bowl several times until compacted. This gives the dumplings the correct texture. (It is best to place bowl in the sink to do this.)

3. Using scissors, trim won ton wrappers to form circles.

4. For each dumpling, place wrapper in your slightly cupped hand, then place about 1 tablespoon filling in center of wrapper.

5. Gather up edges of wrapper around filling to form pleats. Lightly squeeze the center to form a waist, then tap bottom on surface to flatten. With a spoon, push filling into

wrapper, smoothing the top. Place a piece of diced pepper or a coriander leaf on the surface of dumpling. Make the remaining dumplings in the same manner.

6. Lightly oil the bottom of a heatproof dish (I use a Pyrex pie plate), arrange dumplings on it, leaving a space in between to allow steam to circulate. Do in batches if necessary.

7. Place a rack in wok; fill with water to bottom edge of rack. Cover; bring to a boil. Place dumplings in dish on rack over boiling water, cover, and steam 8 minutes or until cooked through. Serve hot with Worcestershire sauce and chili sauce.

Makes about 40 dumplings.

GARLIC STEAMED OYSTERS

I had always believed that the only way to eat oysters was raw, on the half shell with absolutely no embellishments, until I was served these garlicky jewels at a banquet in Chinatown. I've since enjoyed them many times in local Chinese restaurants where they're always made with Pacific oysters. I find these a tad too large and strongly flavored for my taste (if you like them, do use them, but be sure to make a lot more sauce to cover them) so I decided to try the dish with my favorite malpeques instead. Try using your own favorite oyster, but because they shrink somewhat in size once steamed, be sure to use only plump ones. This is a very simple dish — though timing is everything. The oysters must not be overcooked and the garlic seasoning must be ready at the instant the oysters are. To eat, just pick up the shell and either use chopsticks for the oyster or slurp in every glorious garlicky mouthful.

8 medium-size fresh oysters
3 tablespoons vegetable oil
6 large garlic cloves, minced
1 tablespoon sesame oil

1. Thoroughly scrub oysters under cold running water. Open them; leave on the half shell, severing oyster from the muscle with a sharp knife while taking care not to lose oyster liquor from the shell.

2. Arrange oysters — carefully so as not to spill oyster liquor — on a heatproof dish such as a Pyrex pie plate.

3. Place a rack in wok; fill with water to bottom edge of rack. Cover; bring to a boil. Place dish containing oysters on rack, cover, and steam for 5 minutes or until just cooked through. Do not overcook.

4. Meanwhile, about 2 minutes before oysters are ready, heat vegetable oil in a small nonstick skillet on high heat. When hot, add garlic and cook until tender, about 1 minute. Be careful not to let garlic brown. Stir in sesame oil; remove skillet from heat. The mixture must be sizzling hot.

5. Remove lid from wok; immediately spoon about 1 teaspoon garlic mixture over each oyster. Remove dish containing oysters from steamer and either serve from the dish or transfer oysters to a more attractive, heated serving platter. Serve at once.

Serves 2 to 4.

A cook prepares six soup orders simultaneously (garnishing with one hand while deftly shooting sesame oil into a bowl with the other) as the waitress snatches the completed dishes.

SOUPS

SOUP STOCK

I once worked briefly in a Chinese restaurant kitchen. While there, I learned many cooking secrets, one being the secret of a good soup stock. The stockpot was always simmering on the back burner and the cooks continually tossed in bones and meat scraps from pork, chicken, and duck — even chicken feet and shrimp shells. This makes a stock that is not only delicious, but blends well with a variety of poultry, meat, or seafood soups and sauces. I have experimented with many stocks using chicken and pork bones, but — like the average home cook — I simply never have the volume of bones available that a restaurant has, and so these stocks lacked the fullness of flavor I sought. I finally found that the best homemade stock needs a whole chicken, spareribs or pork bones, and shrimp shells — or several whole, unpeeled shrimp. Stock will keep in the refrigerator for 4 to 5 days, but then it must be reboiled or frozen.

1 roasting chicken, about 4 pounds
1 pound spareribs or pork bones
2 ounces shrimp shells (from ½ pound shrimp)
2 quarter-size slices fresh ginger
4 large green onions, left whole
1 celery stalk, cut into three pieces
2 teaspoons salt
¼ cup dry sherry (optional)
14 cups water

1. Remove fat from cavity of chicken. Rinse chicken under cold running water — including the inside cavity. This helps keep the stock clear. Using a very heavy cleaver and rubber mallet, chop the chicken through the bones, into 2- to 3-inch pieces. Cut the spareribs between each rib or chop up the pork bones.

2. Place all the ingredients in a large, heavy pot. Bring to a boil, reduce heat to low, and simmer, skimming off foam with a fine-mesh skimmer until clear (about 10 minutes).

3. Simmer stock, uncovered, for a minimum of 2 hours (for a light broth), and up to 4 hours for a rich-flavored broth. Taste for seasoning and add salt to taste.

4. Strain stock through a colander or large strainer; discard the meat, bones, and vegetables. For very clear broth, line a strainer with cheesecloth that has first been rinsed and wrung out, then pour in the broth, letting it strain through.

5. Refrigerate stock uncovered (do not cover until cooled or the stock will turn sour). Once the stock is cooled, the fat will have risen to the top and half of it can be removed. Don't remove all of it, though, or the stock will lose flavor.

Makes about 10 cups.

BEEF AND EGGDROP SOUP

T his classic, nourishing soup has a fresh, immediate flavor heightened by fragrant ripe tomatoes, pungent coriander, and the spicy aroma of freshly ground black pepper. Reduce the amount of pepper by half if you don't want the soup too peppery hot, but put the peppermill on the table for those who want to add more. I find this soup tastes best when freshly made, but it can be made up to a day ahead. Don't add coriander (or green onion) until just before serving. For an informal supper, pair it with Pot Stickers (page 18).

½ pound ground beef
2 teaspoons soy sauce
4 cups water
4 cups soup (page 34) or chicken
   stock
2 tablespoons finely chopped
   fresh ginger
1 large ripe tomato, diced
1 tablespoon soy sauce
1 tablespoon dry sherry
1 teaspoon freshly ground
   black pepper
Salt

THICKENER
Combine in small bowl:
3 tablespoons potato or cornstarch
3 tablespoons water

1 egg, lightly beaten with ¼ teaspoon
   sesame oil
1 tablespoon sesame oil
¼ cup coarsely chopped fresh
   coriander *or* 2 large green onions,
   finely chopped

1. Combine beef and soy sauce in bowl; set aside to marinate while water boils.

2. Bring water to a boil in medium saucepan. Add beef to boiling water; blanch beef (cook a few seconds), stirring with chopsticks to break up lumps. Drain beef in a strainer; discard water.

3. Rinse saucepan; return to high heat. Add soup or chicken stock and ginger; bring to a boil on high heat. Reduce heat to simmer; add blanched beef, tomato, soy sauce, dry sherry, pepper, and salt to taste. Simmer for 5 minutes.

4. Restir *thickener;* pour into soup. Turn heat to high; bring to a boil, and stir until slightly thickened. Remove from heat.

5. Slowly pour beaten egg into soup in a thin stream, stirring gently with a chopstick. Drizzle in sesame oil. Sprinkle in coriander *or* green onions, taste for seasoning, and transfer to a soup tureen or divide among individual bowls.

Serves 4 to 6.

SHRIMP WON TON SOUP

Without a doubt, won ton soup is the most popular Chinese soup in America. Most restaurants serve pork-stuffed won tons or a combination of pork and shrimp because it's cheaper than using all shrimp. But all-shrimp won tons are not only tastier, they are much prettier and more elegant: I like the way the pink shrimp and green onion colors show through the wrappers, once cooked. Do not chop the shrimp in a food processor: it will become a paste. Instead, for the best texture, dice the shrimp the size of large peas. Pair won ton soup with an appetizer such as Green Onion Cakes (page 27) or Spring Rolls (page 17) for a delightful light meal. Won tons become wonderful preprandial nibbles when deep-fried. To make, stuff wrappers, then heat oil to 350°F. Deep-fry for 2 to 3 minutes or until golden. Serve with Sweet and Sour Sauce (page 74), and chilled champagne or Chinese beer. The won tons are hot; reduce chili oil by half for less heat but don't omit altogether.

1 pound raw shrimp, peeled, deveined, and diced

SEASONINGS
½ teaspoon salt
¼ teaspoon sugar
1 tablespoon sesame oil
1 teaspoon dry sherry
2 teaspoons chili oil
1 large egg white
1 tablespoon finely chopped fresh ginger
1 whole green onion, finely chopped
2 tablespoons diced bamboo shoots
2 teaspoons potato or cornstarch

1 package thin won ton wrappers
6 cups soup (page 34) or chicken stock
2 tablespoons finely chopped fresh ginger
2 tablespoons dry sherry
1 tablespoon sesame oil
Chopped fresh coriander or green onions (garnish)

1. Combine shrimp and *seasonings* in medium bowl.

2. Bring 8 cups water to a boil in large pot while stuffing won tons.

3. Hold a won ton wrapper in palm of one hand. Take about 1 teaspoon filling and place in center of wrapper. Bring sides of wrapper up to cover filling and squeeze and pinch top to seal. They will look like tiny pouches. Tap bottom gently about 5 times while pinching top, turn and pinch, tap, turn, and pinch to pack filling. Place on large plate or tray and continue until all are filled.

4. Drop won tons in boiling water, pinching top once more to seal as you add them. Cook for 2 minutes or until cooked through, stirring gently

with chopsticks to prevent them sticking to bottom of pot. Do not overcook. Remove won tons with a Chinese strainer or slotted spoon.

5. Portion them into serving bowls (4 to 6 won tons per person for a soup course, 6 to 10 as a meal or snack) or serve from a tureen.

6. Meanwhile, bring stock, ginger, and dry sherry to a boil in medium saucepan. Reduce heat to low, drizzle in sesame oil, and pour over won tons. Garnish with coriander or green onions. Serve at once.

Makes about 44 won tons.

Won ton soup is among the most satisfying of Chinatown soups. My version is made more exquisite by using shrimp instead of the usual pork-stuffed dumplings.

A wonderfully fresh-tasting bowl of soup featuring fresh tomatoes, ginger, and chicken is served with crispy won tons and their dipping sauce (page 36).

CHICKEN WITH FRESH TOMATO AND GINGER SOUP

T his is a light, bright, easy-to-make soup with tender chicken shreds, fresh ripe tomatoes, and coriander floating in a refreshing gingery broth. For me, fresh coriander makes this soup come alive, but it's also quite tasty with green onions. Most people are surprised to find tomatoes in Chinese cooking. They're not native to China but the Cantonese, especially, enjoy them in such dishes as stir-fried beef and tomatoes or diced in soups such as this one.

2 chicken breast halves (about 1 pound), skinned, boned, and sliced into shreds

MARINADE
2 tablespoons water
1 teaspoon soy sauce
1 teaspoon dry sherry
¼ teaspoon sesame oil
1 teaspoon potato or cornstarch

4 cups soup (page 34) or chicken stock
2 tablespoons finely chopped fresh ginger
2 medium tomatoes, cut into large dice
2 tablespoons dry sherry
½ teaspoon salt
¼ teaspoon freshly ground black pepper
¼ cup chopped fresh coriander *or* 3 green onions, finely chopped
1 tablespoon sesame oil

1. Combine chicken and *marinade* in bowl; marinate while bringing stock to a boil.

2. Bring soup or chicken stock to a boil in medium saucepan. Reduce heat; add ginger and simmer for 5 minutes. Add chicken and tomatoes. Stir gently to separate chicken shreds; cook for 2 minutes or until chicken is cooked through.

3. Add dry sherry, salt, pepper, coriander or green onions, and sesame oil; stir. Serve immediately.

Serves 4.

PORK AND SZECHUAN PRESERVED VEGETABLE SOUP

Chili oil lends heat and fragrance to this simple Szechuan soup chock-full of shredded pork, tangy mustard green, black mushrooms, and crunchy bamboo shoots. Because the preserved mustard green is salty and pungent, many recipes suggest rinsing off the chili powder coating but I don't find it necessary. Szechuan preserved vegetable is available in cans in Oriental food shops. Once the can is opened, transfer to a clean glass jar with a lid and refrigerate. This way, it will last several months.

¼ pound pork tenderloin, cut into matchstick-size shreds

MARINADE
1 teaspoon soy sauce
1 teaspoon dry sherry
½ teaspoon sesame oil
¼ teaspoon potato or cornstarch

5 cups soup (page 34) or chicken stock
1 tablespoon finely chopped fresh ginger
2 ounces bean thread noodles, soaked for 30 seconds in hot water, drained, and, using scissors, cut into 4-inch lengths
2 Chinese dried black mushrooms, stems snapped off, caps soaked for 30 minutes in hot water, squeezed dry, and thinly sliced
¼ cup matchstick-size shreds preserved mustard green
⅓ cup matchstick-size shreds bamboo shoots
1 tablespoon sesame oil
1 tablespoon chili oil
½ cup coarsely chopped fresh coriander

. . . .

1. Combine pork and *marinade* in bowl; set aside to marinate while preparing remaining ingredients.

2. Bring soup or chicken stock to a boil in a medium saucepan. Reduce heat to simmer; add pork and ginger, stirring with chopsticks to separate shreds. Cook for 2 minutes. Add noodles, mushrooms, mustard green, and bamboo shoots; simmer another 2 minutes. Add sesame oil, chili oil, and coriander. To serve, use chopsticks to portion the noodles into bowls, then ladle in meat, vegetables, and broth.

Serves 4.

HOT AND SOUR SOUP

Fiery hot with volatile chili oil, ginger, and fragrant black pepper; slightly sour from the addition of vinegar; textured with crunchy vegetables, tender pork shreds, and "egg flowers," this may seem an unorthodox combination. Once tasted, though, it's easy to see why this hearty soup with its complex blending of flavors and heat, is so popular in American Chinatowns. As a variation, add 1 cake bean curd, diced, and ¼ cup julienned carrot. If you make this soup ahead of time, don't add seasoning liquid until just before serving.

¼ pound pork tenderloin, cut into matchstick-size shreds

MARINADE
¼ teaspoon salt
⅛ teaspoon sugar
Pinch white pepper
½ teaspoon dry sherry
½ teaspoon sesame oil

4 cups soup (page 34) or chicken stock
1 tablespoon finely chopped fresh ginger
½ cup matchstick-size shreds bamboo shoots
¼ cup dried lily buds, soaked in cold water for 20 minutes, squeezed dry, hard parts cut off
3 large Chinese dried black mushrooms, stems snapped off, caps soaked for 30 minutes in hot water, squeezed dry, and thinly sliced
2 large tree ears, soaked in hot water for 20 minutes, knobby parts cut off, sliced into thin julienne

SEASONING LIQUID
Combine in bowl:
3 tablespoons cider vinegar
2 tablespoons soy sauce
1 tablespoon sesame oil
1 tablespoon chili oil
½ teaspoon freshly ground black pepper
2 tablespoons potato starch

1 large egg, lightly beaten

•   •   •   •   •   •   •   •   •   •   •

1. Combine pork and *marinade* in bowl; set aside to marinate while preparing other ingredients.

2. Bring soup or chicken stock to a boil in medium saucepan. Reduce heat to simmer; add pork and ginger, stirring with chopsticks to separate pork shreds, and cook for 2 minutes. Add everything except *seasoning liquid*; bring to a boil. Restir *seasoning liquid* and pour into soup.

Stir until thickened; remove from heat (soup must not continue to boil once vinegar is added). Slowly pour beaten egg into soup in a thin stream, stirring gently with a chopstick to form "egg flowers." Taste and adjust seasoning if necessary, with extra vinegar, pepper, or chili oil. Serve immediately.

Serves 4.

Stacks of bowls sit on the counter of a tiny "take-away" noodle stand.

RICE AND NOODLES

WHITE RICE

M any people say they find it difficult to make simple boiled rice — usually meaning that it's sticky, when they want it to be al dente. They may not realize that the Chinese prefer rice that way: light, tender, and slightly sticky so that it's easy to pick up with chopsticks. The Chinese prefer long-grain white rice. Never use "converted" (parboiled) or instant rice because they just don't have the correct texture or flavor. The exact ratio of rice to water is tricky: some people do prefer it to be firmer than others. But I have found an almost foolproof method that Chinese cooks use to produce perfectly cooked rice every time. They never measure rice and water; instead, the rice is simply covered with 1 inch of water. I use an automatic rice cooker: it not only frees a burner for other uses, it automatically shuts off when the rice is cooked, and will keep it warm for an hour or more. Rice cookers are available in Chinatown food shops and hardware stores. The following recipe makes enough rice for 4 rice-loving people (an average of 2 rice bowls each) or make Fried Rice (page 46) with any that's left over.

2 cups long-grain white rice
3½ cups water

1. Place rice in a strainer; wash thoroughly by rinsing under cold running water, swirling rice with your hands several times, until the water runs clear.

2. Place washed, drained rice and water in heavy 2½ quart saucepan. Do not stir.

3. Bring water to a boil on high heat. Cover; reduce heat to low and simmer for 20 minutes. Turn off heat; let sit undisturbed for 10 minutes more. Do *not* uncover saucepan during simmering and standing period. The rice, if kept covered, will keep warm up to 30 minutes. When ready to serve, uncover, but do not "fluff" the rice before serving it.

Serves 4 to 6.

ANTS CLIMBING A TREE

The Chinese have a much greater variety of noodle dishes than anyone else — even more than the pasta-loving Italians. Chinese noodles, both fresh and dried, are produced from many different kinds of grains — mung bean flour, rice flour, seaweed starch, and wheat to name a few —yet are always served long because in Chinese culture, noodles are a symbol of longevity. That's why they are traditionally served on birthdays and devoured uncut or unbroken. However, the humble noodle is not only birthday food, but an ordinary staple enjoyed by everyone. This noodle dish, with its fanciful name, is so called because the little bits of pork supposedly resemble ants climbing on tree branches (the dark noodles). Not only am I fond of the name, I adore the textural quality of the bean thread noodles — which could be described as both slippery and delicately elastic — and the wonderful way they absorb the chili-spiked seasonings. This dish can be prepared in advance and reheated gently. If doing this, be sure to separate noodles, if in a clump, place them in a heavy saucepan or casserole, add about 1 tablespoon of chicken stock, and cook over low heat, covered, or in a 350°F oven, for 10 minutes or until heated through.

6 ounces ground pork

MARINADE
1 tablespoon soy sauce
1 tablespoon dry sherry
1 teaspoon sesame oil
¼ teaspoon freshly ground black pepper
1 teaspoon potato or cornstarch

Oil for stir-frying
3 large garlic cloves, chopped
4 whole green onions, chopped
4 teaspoons chili paste with soy bean
4 ounces bean thread (cellophane) noodles, soaked for 20 minutes in hot water (no longer) and drained

SEASONING LIQUID
Combine in bowl:
⅔ cup chicken stock
1 teaspoon sugar
2 teaspoons dry sherry
4 teaspoons soy sauce
¼ teaspoon sesame oil

A few sprigs fresh coriander or chopped green onion (garnish)

•   •   •   •   •   •   •   •   •

1. Combine pork and *marinade* in bowl; marinate for 30 minutes or up to 24 hours, covered, in refrigerator.

2. Heat wok on high heat. Add 2 tablespoons oil; when hot, add garlic and green onions and cook for a few seconds. Add chili paste and pork; stir-fry, breaking up lumps at the same time, until meat is no longer pink. Add noodles; stir to blend.

3. Pour in *seasoning liquid;* bring to a boil. Cover, cook on high heat (lifting lid to stir occasionally) for 3 minutes or until noodles absorb stock. Do not overcook noodles or they will turn mushy. Remove to a heated serving platter and garnish with coriander or green onion. To serve, use chopsticks to untangle and portion the slippery noodles.

Serves 4.

RAINBOW FRIED RICE

Here's a colorful, fresh-tasting variation of the ever-popular Chinatown staple. In the Orient, fried rice is eaten as a snack or as a meal in itself with soup, not in place of steamed rice as it's often served in American restaurants. The secret of excellent fried rice is to use only cold rice, so that it doesn't absorb too much oil when fried. And in order to keep the vibrant colors of the individual ingredients, you shouldn't add soy sauce or oyster sauce. I have listed them as an option for those of you who will hunger for that familiar Chinatown seasoning and hue, but do taste this rice first to see if you like it without these additions. It is best when freshly made, but you can prepare the rice ahead of time and reheat by adding about 1 tablespoon oil to a heated wok or nonstick skillet, then stir-frying for 2 to 3 minutes or until heated through.

2 to 3 tablespoons vegetable oil
2 large eggs, well beaten with
 ½ teaspoon sesame oil
2 large garlic cloves, chopped
1 tablespoon finely chopped
 fresh ginger
3 large whole green onions, chopped
1 small sweet red pepper, seeds
 removed and diced
8 Chinese dried black mushrooms,
 stems snapped off, caps soaked in
 hot water for 30 minutes, squeezed
 dry, and thinly sliced
16 snow peas, ends trimmed, sliced
 into julienne
½ cup fresh or frozen peas
2 to 3 ounces Chinese barbecued
 pork, fat trimmed and thinly sliced
 or 1 Chinese sausage, steamed (see
 Glossary) and thinly sliced
½ pound small raw shrimp, peeled
 and deveined

4 cups cold cooked rice
2 tablespoons chicken stock
 (optional)
½ teaspoon salt
2 tablespoons oyster sauce (optional)
1 tablespoon soy sauce (optional)

. . . .

1. Heat 2 teaspoons oil in wok. Pour in beaten eggs; tilt wok to distribute egg into a thin pancake. Cook for 1 to 2 minutes or until just set — no need to flip over. Remove to a plate; cut into thin julienne.

2. Heat wok on high heat. Add 1 tablespoon oil; when hot, add garlic, ginger, green onions, red pepper, mushrooms, snow peas, and peas. Stir-fry for 1 minute or until heated through. Add pork or sausage and shrimp; toss for 1 minute or until shrimp turn pink. Add rice, breaking up any lumps with hands before adding, and continue tossing for about 1 to 2 minutes or until mixed and heated through. Add a little more oil if rice is sticking to wok. If not using oyster and soy sauce, and rice seems too dry, add a little stock if necessary and continue tossing. Sprinkle in salt.

3. Taste for seasoning and add oyster sauce and/or soy sauce if using. Toss in egg shreds; stir until combined.

Serves 4 to 6.

Leftover rice becomes a flavorful new dish when seafood, meat, and vegetables are added.

Chow mein, in Chinese, simply means fried noodles.

CHOW MEIN

C how mein, the ubiquitous Chinatown fried noodle dish, is enormously popular with its combination of colors, textures, and tastes. I think you'll find my rendition more elegant and bountiful than the Chinatown version because I combine shrimp and chicken with brilliant snow peas and sweet red peppers along with crunchy fresh water chestnuts, chewy tree ears, and black mushrooms. The ingredients are infinitely variable, so feel free to experiment by substituting broccoli or Chinese cabbage, for example, or pork, beef, or squid. I often fry the noodles a few hours in advance, then set them aside. Just before serving, place them on a serving platter in a 350°F oven for 5 minutes to reheat before completing dish. Don't leave the noodles in the oven too long or they will dry out. To eat chow mein, each person lifts out a portion of noodles with their chopsticks (the trick is to be slightly aggressive when tackling the tangle of noodles and lift them out and up), places them on their dinner plate or in their rice bowl, and then nabs a few pieces of chicken or shrimp and vegetables.

1 chicken breast half (about ½ pound), skinned, boned, cut in half lengthwise, then thinly sliced on the diagonal

MARINADE
1 tablespoon water
¼ teaspoon soy sauce
¼ teaspoon dry sherry
¼ teaspoon sesame oil
½ teaspoon potato or cornstarch

½ pound raw shrimp, peeled and deveined

MARINADE
¼ teaspoon salt
⅛ teaspoon sugar
Pinch white pepper
1½ teaspoons dry sherry
½ teaspoon sesame oil
½ teaspoon potato or cornstarch

Oil for stir-frying
½ pound fresh chow mein noodles,

placed in strainer in sink, a kettle-full of boiling water poured over them, drained, then tossed with 1 tablespoon sesame oil
3 large garlic cloves, chopped
1 tablespoon finely chopped fresh ginger
6 Chinese dried black mushrooms, stems snapped off, caps soaked for 30 minutes in hot water, squeezed dry, and thinly sliced
1 large tree ear, soaked for 20 minutes in hot water, knobby parts cut off, sliced into thick julienne
4 fresh water chestnuts, peeled and sliced in half
2 rings sweet red pepper, diced
6 snow peas, ends trimmed
2 large whole green onions, chopped

SEASONING LIQUID
Combine in bowl:
1 cup chicken stock
2 tablespoons hoisin sauce
1 tablespoon dry sherry

(seasoning liquid continued)
1 tablespoon soy sauce
2 teaspoons sesame oil
½ teaspoon sugar

THICKENER
Combine in small bowl:
2 tablespoons potato or cornstarch
2 tablespoons water

. . . .

1. Combine chicken and *marinade* in bowl; marinate 30 minutes or up to 24 hours, covered, in refrigerator.

2. Combine shrimp and *marinade* in bowl; marinate 30 minutes or up to 6 hours, covered, in refrigerator.

3. Preheat oven to 350°F. Place large (13-inch) heatproof platter in oven.

4. Heat 10-inch nonstick or cast iron

skillet on high heat. Add 2 tablespoons oil; when hot, add noodles and press into a round pancake shape. Fry noodles for 2 to 3 minutes each side or until both sides are golden brown and crisp, flipping over noodle "pancake" and adding more oil if needed by lifting noodle cake and pouring underneath. Remove to the heated serving platter; put back in oven to keep warm.

5. Heat wok on high heat. Add 3 tablespoons oil; when hot, add chicken. Stir-fry for 2 to 3 minutes or until opaque. Remove to plate. Add shrimp; stir-fry for 1 to 2 minutes or until pink. Remove to plate with chicken.

6. Clean and dry wok if charred bits stick to bottom. Return to high heat. Add 2 to 3 tablespoons oil; when hot, add garlic and ginger and cook a few seconds. Add mushrooms, tree ears, water chestnuts, red pepper, snow peas, and green onions; toss for 1 minute or until heated through. Return chicken and shrimp to wok; toss to mix.

7. Pour in *seasoning liquid;* bring to

a boil. Restir *thickener,* pour into wok and stir until thickened.

8. Remove platter from oven; top noodles with mixture. Serve at once.

Serves 4 to 6.

. . . .

SINGAPORE NOODLES

W onderful curry-flavored rice stick noodles combined with seafood, meat, egg strips, and crisp vegetables are justifiably popular in Cantonese restaurants and noodle houses in Chinatown. Curry is not a seasoning that is usually associated with Chinese cuisine: this noodle dish made its way from Singapore to Southern China. Like most noodle dishes, this one makes an excellent one-dish meal and is also great for a snack or lunch. It can be prepared in advance and reheated by adding about 1 tablespoon oil to heated wok or large nonstick skillet, and stir-frying for 2 minutes or until heated through.

½ pound raw shrimp, peeled and deveined

MARINADE
¼ teaspoon salt
⅛ teaspoon sugar
⅛ teaspoon white pepper
1½ teaspoons dry sherry
½ teaspoon sesame oil
½ teaspoon potato or cornstarch

6 ounces rice stick (rice vermicelli) noodles
Oil for stir-frying
1 egg, well beaten with ¼ teaspoon sesame oil
1 carrot, cut into fine julienne
1 medium onion, cut into wedges (eighths)
1 tablespoon water
2 cups bean sprouts
6 ounces Chinese barbecued pork, fat trimmed, and cut into matchstick-size shreds
¼ teaspoon sugar
1 teaspoon soy sauce
2 large garlic cloves, chopped
1 tablespoon finely chopped fresh ginger

SEASONING LIQUID
Combine in bowl:
¼ cup chicken stock
2 tablespoons dry sherry
1 tablespoon soy sauce
1 tablespoon curry powder
1 teaspoon sugar
½ teaspoon salt

1 large whole green onion, shredded
1 tablespoon toasted sesame seeds (garnish)

1. Combine shrimp and *marinade* in bowl; marinate for 30 minutes or up to 6 hours, covered, in refrigerator.

2. Place noodles in heatproof bowl, pour boiling water over them and allow to soak for 30 seconds, then drain immediately. Do not soak longer or they will be too soft. When cool enough to handle, use fingers or chopsticks to untangle noodles. Cover with plastic wrap; set aside.

3. Heat medium nonstick skillet or wok on high heat. Add 1 teaspoon oil to coat bottom. Add beaten egg; tilt skillet or wok to spread egg into a thin pancake. Cook egg 1 minute or until set. Remove to a plate, slice into shreds, and set aside for garnish.

4. Clean wok; return to high heat. Add 1 tablespoon oil; when hot, add carrot and onion. Toss a few seconds; add 1 tablespoon water, cover, and steam-cook for 1 to 2 minutes or until tender. Remove to a plate; set aside.

5. Add another tablespoon of oil to wok if necessary. Add bean sprouts; stir-fry for about 30 seconds or until just wilted but still crisp. Remove immediately; set aside with carrot and onion.

6. Add a little more oil if necessary; when hot, add barbecued pork, ¼ teaspoon sugar, and 1 teaspoon soy sauce. Toss a few seconds to heat

through. Remove; set aside with carrot and onion.

7. Add a little more oil if necessary, then garlic, ginger, and shrimp. Stir-fry for 1 minute or until they turn pink.

8. Return cooked ingredients to wok. Restir *seasoning liquid;* pour into wok. Place noodles on top of vegetables, untangling as you add them, but don't mix with meat and vegetables.

9. Cover; steam-cook 1 minute or until noodles are tender. Remove lid; toss with chopsticks in one hand and wooden spatula in the other to combine ingredients.

10. Add green onions; toss and transfer to a large heated platter. Sprinkle with sesame seeds and garnish with egg shreds.

Serves 6.

TALKING NOODLES

T he Chinese do not share our Western view that boisterous activity during mealtime is impolite. The pleasures of eating are very important to them as is evident when dining in Chinatown. The clatter of dishes and sounds of families — which include everyone from babies to Grandma and Grandpa — are sometimes unbelievably loud. And to add to the fun, the Chinese have created numerous dishes which produce sounds: sizzling rice soup (hot rice cakes dropped into hot soup); sizzling platters (stir-fried meat placed on very hot iron plates and served sputtering and crackling); and this recipe where the noodles crackle and crunch, "talking" as the server stirs to combine the meat mixture with them.

3 ounces rice stick (rice vermicelli) noodles
3 cups vegetable oil for deep-frying
½ pound ground pork

MARINADE
1 teaspoon soy sauce
2 teaspoons dry sherry
½ teaspoon sesame oil
½ teaspoon potato or cornstarch

1 large iceberg lettuce
4 large garlic cloves, chopped
1 tablespoon finely chopped fresh ginger
6 Chinese dried black mushrooms, stems removed, caps soaked for 30 minutes in hot water, squeezed dry, and diced
2 large whole green onions, chopped
1 medium carrot, finely chopped (about ½ cup)
1 small celery stalk, finely chopped (about ⅓ cup)
2 tablespoons hoisin sauce

SPREADING SAUCE
Combine in small bowl:
4 tablespoons hoisin sauce
4 tablespoons plum sauce

1. Separate noodles and break them into pieces about 4 inches long (this is best done in the sink because they tend to fly all over the place).

2. Heat wok on high heat. Add oil; heat to 375° F. Deep-fry noodles for a few seconds, in 3 batches, until they puff up and turn pure white. Do not brown. Remove immediately to a paper towel-lined plate to drain, then place on a serving platter. (You may prepare the noodles several hours ahead and set them aside, uncovered, at room temperature.)

3. Combine pork and marinade in bowl; marinate for 30 minutes or up to 6 hours, covered, in refrigerator.

4. Separate 8 lettuce leaves, stack them inside each other, place in a plastic bag, and refrigerate until ready to use. Just before serving, place them on a serving dish.

5. Heat wok on high heat. Add 2 tablespoons oil; when hot, add garlic and ginger and cook a few seconds. Add pork; stir-fry, breaking up lumps until cooked through. Add chopped vegetables; toss for 1 minute or until tender-crisp. Stir in hoisin sauce; toss until mixed.

6. Scoop out mixture and carefully place on top of fried noodles, leaving a border of noodles around the edge.

7. To serve, bring the platter of pork-noodle mixture, dish of lettuce cups, and spreading sauce to the table. Using a serving spoon and a dinner fork, very carefully and gently turn the meat mixture, while at the same time cutting the noodles to mix the ingredients. Do not overmix.

8. To eat, each person takes a lettuce leaf, spoons some spreading sauce on it, then some meat-noodle mixture, finally rolling the lettuce to encase the meat mixture, and eating it with the hands.

Makes 8 lettuce cups.

A filling of ground pork, diced vegetables, and crunchy noodles is rolled into a crisp lettuce leaf to form a Chinese-style sandwich.

On the sidewalk, iced fresh fish for sale.

FISH AND SEAFOOD

A platter of lobster is both dazzling and delicious — fun and messy to eat.

LOBSTER CANTONESE

Beautiful bright red lobsters first steamed or boiled, then stir-fried with plenty of garlic, ginger, fermented black beans, and my own addition of grated lemon zest combine to create an exquisite taste experience. Most recipes for this dish include ground pork and egg whites in the sauce but I've omitted them in order to enhance the delicate flavor of the lobster. Typically, Chinese chefs cut lobsters up while they are still alive. I'm afraid I can't do that: I find it traumatic enough to plunge the lobsters headfirst into boiling water — supposedly the most humane way of dispatching them. Although best if steamed or boiled, cut up, and stir-fried immediately, the lobster can be cooked up to a day ahead, covered, refrigerated, then brought back to room temperature before chopping and stir-frying. For a very simple dinner, I serve this dish with white rice or Rainbow Fried Rice (page 46) and a vegetable. It's fun to share this meal with convivial friends who don't mind getting their hands messy while extracting the lobster meat with chopsticks and fingers — but do provide finger bowls and lots of paper napkins!

Water for steaming or boiling
Salt
2 live lobsters (1 to 1½ pounds each)
2 tablespoons vegetable oil
6 quarter-size slices fresh ginger, shredded
5 large garlic cloves, thinly sliced
1 tablespoon fermented black beans, coarsely chopped
Grated zest of 1 medium lemon

SEASONING LIQUID
Combine in bowl:
¼ cup chicken stock
1 tablespoon dry sherry
1 teaspoon oyster sauce
½ teaspoon sugar

THICKENER
Combine in small bowl:
1 teaspoon potato or cornstarch
2 teaspoons water

5 whole green onions, shredded
1 teaspoon sesame oil

1. *To steam lobsters:* pour 2 inches of water into a large pot or steamer; add a little salt. Place lobsters in pot. Cover; bring to a boil and steam for about 12 minutes. Turn off heat but keep covered and let the lobsters sit for 5 minutes in the hot water. *To boil lobsters:* bring a large pot of water to a boil; add about 2 to 3 teaspoons of salt per quart of water. Plunge lobsters, headfirst, and one at a time, into the boiling water. Cover; cook for 10 to 12 minutes or until just cooked through. Do not overcook.

2. Immediately remove lobsters; place in sink or large bowl. When cool enough to handle, place on a cutting surface.

3. Twist off tails, and using a heavy cleaver or large chef's knife (and a rubber mallet if necessary), cut the tail into 3 or 4 sections. Twist off the arms, then break the claws away from arms. Using the flat side of cleaver (and covering with dish towel to prevent splattering), smash the claws and arms in several places to crack them. (This allows the sauce to penetrate and makes it easier to remove the lobster meat.) Remove and set aside legs, then cut through the undershell of the lobster lengthwise, splitting it in two. Extract and discard the stomach sac — a 1-inch long pouch in the head — but be careful not to disturb the green tomalley (liver) and any (red) roe. Place lobster parts in a large bowl.

4. Heat wok on high heat. Add oil;

when hot, add ginger, garlic, black beans, and lemon zest and stir for 30 seconds. Add lobster pieces; toss for 30 seconds to coat with seasonings.

5. Restir *seasoning liquid;* pour

down side of wok and immediately cover. Steam-cook for 1 minute or until lobster is heated through. Do not overcook.

6. Uncover wok; restir *thickener* and add to wok. Toss for 30 seconds or until thickened. Add green onions,

toss, then drizzle in sesame oil. Toss briskly to combine; scoop out and place on a heated platter.

Serves 2 to 4.

. . . .

CRISPY SHRIMP IN SPICY SALT

I've enjoyed these salty, crunchy shrimp many times in our local Chinatown. The shrimp are first deep-fried, then stir-fried in a mixture of spicy salt and, believe it or not, you can then eat them shell and all! Be sure the oil is hot enough and that it remains hot throughout deep-frying; otherwise the shells will not be crisp enough to be edible. Also the shrimp must not be large or the shells will be too tough. If the idea of eating the shell bothers you or your dinner companions, by all means peel the shrimp — they are still absolutely delicious finger food.

½ pound raw medium shrimp in shell, no more than 3 inches in length
⅓ cup cornstarch
2 cups vegetable oil for deep-frying
1 teaspoon spicy salt

1. Do not remove shells from shrimp. Put cornstarch on wax paper; coat each shrimp thoroughly.

2. Heat wok on high heat. Add oil; heat to 400°F. Deep-fry shrimp in 2 batches, for about 1 minute or until shells are crisp (remove after 1 minute and test one to see). Do not overcook. Remove each batch to a paper towel-lined plate to drain.

3. Pour out all but 1 tablespoon oil; return wok to high heat. Return shrimp to wok and add spicy salt. Toss shrimp and seasoning for about 30 seconds to let seasoning permeate shrimp. Transfer to a heated serving dish.

Serves 2 to 4.

HUNAN HOT AND GARLICKY SHRIMP

Many people are amazed to find the ubiquitous ketchup used as a seasoning in Asian cooking and tend to ask if this use is authentic. The word "ketchup" or "catsup" comes from the Malayan word "kechap" (fish sauce) which comes from the Chinese "ke-tsiap", but it is not known if the actual tomato-based sauce originated in Asia. Not readily available here, there is a ketchup manufactured in Hong Kong that is very similar in taste to the North American version, but your own favorite brand will definitely do. Ketchup combined with garlic, ginger, and other Chinese seasonings is a wonderful sweet-tasting combination that is most often coupled with shrimp or seafood, or with deep-fried spareribs.

1 pound raw shrimp, peeled and deveined

MARINADE
½ teaspoon salt
¼ teaspoon sugar
⅛ teaspoon white pepper
1 tablespoon dry sherry
1 teaspoon sesame oil
1 teaspoon potato or cornstarch

2 tablespoons vegetable oil
4 large garlic cloves, chopped
1 tablespoon minced fresh ginger

SEASONING LIQUID
Combine in bowl:
1 tablespoon sugar
3 tablespoons ketchup
1 tablespoon dry sherry
1 tablespoon water
1 tablespoon Worcestershire sauce
1 tablespoon chili paste with
  soy bean
1 teaspoon sesame oil

1. Combine shrimp and *marinade* in bowl; marinate 30 minutes or up to 6 hours, covered, in refrigerator.

2. Heat wok on high heat. Add 2 tablespoons oil; when hot, add garlic and ginger. Cook for a few seconds. Add shrimp; stir-fry for 1 minute or until opaque.

3. Pour *seasoning liquid* into wok; toss for 1 minute to allow shrimp to absorb flavor and sauce to thicken. Transfer to a heated serving dish and serve at once.

Serves 4.

LEMON GARLIC SHRIMP

I *adore this fabulously simple, flavorful, and elegant dish. The bright pink, glistening shrimp are perfectly accented with pungent garlic and tangy lemon. The secret is to buy extra-large shrimp in the shell (either fresh or frozen) — and because the sauce is so delicate, only shrimp with a clean, fresh aroma will do.*

1 pound (about 20 to 24) extra-large raw shrimp, peeled, but with tail and first joint of shell intact, and deveined

MARINADE
½ teaspoon salt
¼ teaspoon sugar
⅛ teaspoon white pepper
1 tablespoon dry sherry
1 teaspoon sesame oil
1 teaspoon potato or cornstarch

2 tablespoons vegetable oil
4 very large garlic cloves, chopped

SEASONING LIQUID
Combine in bowl:
2 tablespoons sugar
Grated zest of 1 medium lemon
3 tablespoons fresh lemon juice
1 tablespoon rice vinegar
1 teaspoon sesame oil
¼ teaspoon hot red pepper flakes or chili oil (optional)

1. Combine shrimp and *marinade* in bowl; marinate for 30 minutes or up to 6 hours, covered, in refrigerator.

2. Heat wok on high heat. Add oil; when hot, add garlic and cook a few seconds. Add shrimp; stir-fry for 2 minutes or until opaque, adding more oil if necessary.

3. Restir *seasoning liquid;* pour into wok. Toss for about 1 minute to allow shrimp to glaze and absorb flavor. Transfer to heated serving dish.

Serves 4.

Heavenly, flash-fried, sweet shrimp in a tangy sauce.

The ultimate squid: quickly fried, then sprinkled with spicy salt.

DEEP-FRIED SQUID WITH SPICY SALT

W hen you order this Cantonese dish in Chinatown, you get either a mixture of fresh and dried squid or, as in this version, all fresh squid. (Dried squid must be reconstituted, is quite strongly flavored, and has a wonderful chewy texture which I like, though few non-Chinese seem to.) Squid is available at most fish markets, some supermarkets, and in Chinatown, either frozen in packages or already thawed at the fish counter. I prefer to purchase squid uncleaned because most cleaned squid is sold without the tentacles — the best part! But if you're squeamish about cleaning them, ask your fishmonger to do it for you. Once the cleaning is done, this is a fast dish that requires only a short marination, a dusting of cornstarch, and last minute frying. But be careful not to cook the squid a minute too long or they will become rubbery!

2 pounds squid, cleaned (see Glossary)

MARINADE
1 tablespoon dry sherry
1 egg white, lightly beaten
½ teaspoon salt

1½ cups cornstarch
Oil for deep-frying
½ teaspoon spicy salt, plus extra for dipping

1. Cut open squid bodies; lightly score the inside surface of each with a sharp knife (be careful not to cut through) in a crisscross pattern. Cut scored squid into about 2- by 3-inch squares; set aside with tentacles.

2. Combine squid and *marinade* in bowl; marinate for about 15 minutes — no longer, or the sherry flavor will be too strong.

3. Place cornstarch on a piece of wax paper; coat squid thoroughly in cornstarch.

4. Heat wok on high heat. Add oil; heat to 375° F. Shake off excess cornstarch and deep-fry several pieces at a time for about 1 to 2 minutes or until pale golden. Do not overcook.

5. Remove with a Chinese strainer or slotted spoon to a paper towel-lined plate. Sprinkle lightly with spicy salt; serve immediately with extra spicy salt for dipping.

Serves 2 to 4.

STEAMED FISH WITH GREEN ONIONS AND GINGER

For purity, taste, and texture there is no better way to cook fish than by steaming. Purchase a whole fish — the freshest possible — and have it cleaned (scaled, gills, and innards removed) with the head and tail left on (including the dorsal fin at the top and the caudal fin at the end) for best flavor and presentation. If you are squeamish about serving a whole fish — and I know a few people who are — then you should still purchase a whole fish, but have it filleted on the spot to guarantee freshness. (Don't even think of using frozen fillets for this dish!) Also, remember to adjust cooking time if you've had your fish filleted. In either case, the secret is not to overcook. To perk up the color of the traditional green onion garnish, I often add slivered hot chilies or sweet red or yellow peppers. Steamed fish may be paired with any stir-fried meat or poultry dish, or for an all-fish dinner, serve with Lemon Garlic Shrimp (page 60), and Mussels with Black Bean Sauce (page 67).

1½ pounds whole pickerel, red snapper, trout, or sea bass, cleaned and scaled
1 tablespoon dry sherry
3 tablespoons finely shredded fresh ginger

3 whole green onions, finely shredded

SEASONING LIQUID
Combine in bowl:
3 tablespoons vegetable oil
4 tablespoons soy sauce
1 tablespoon sugar
1 teaspoon sesame oil

1. Rinse and pat fish dry with paper towels. Place in a heatproof dish that will fit in wok (I use a Pyrex pie plate). Rub each side of fish with sherry. Put half the ginger inside the fish. Set aside.

2. Place a rack in wok; fill with water to bottom edge of rack. Cover; bring to a boil.

3. Place the heatproof dish containing the fish on rack over boiling water, cover, and steam for 15 minutes on high heat or until cooked through. The fish is cooked when a sharp knife is easily inserted into the thickest part of fish and it comes out clean. Do not overcook.

4. Using 2 metal spatulas, gently lift fish out of heatproof dish, leaving behind liquid that has accumulated under fish. Place on heated serving platter (the platter must be hot or the fish will cool by serving time). Scatter remaining ginger and green onions on top of fish.

5. Meanwhile, heat *seasoning liquid* until *rapidly* boiling (it must be very hot) in a small saucepan. Drizzle over entire surface of fish and serve immediately.

Serves 4.

The essence of freshness and simplicity, a whole fish steamed and topped with shreds of green onion and sweet peppers.

The versatile black bean sauce gives mussels an earthy fragrance.

MUSSELS WITH BLACK BEAN SAUCE

T ypically, Chinatown restaurants steam mussels until they open, stir-fry them with black bean sauce, and serve them piled in a bowl. Here, the mussels are removed from the shell after steaming and replaced in their shells along with a little sauce, then set attractively on a platter — a technique that I borrowed from a local Chinatown restaurant. Besides making a prettier presentation, mussels prepared in this way are much easier to consume. Another advantage is that the mussels can be steamed ahead of time and the sauce can be prepared ahead, too. To eat, just pick up a shell and devour the mussel in one voluptuous slurp!

2 dozen medium-sized mussels, scrubbed and debearded
2 tablespoons vegetable oil
2 large garlic cloves, thinly sliced (not chopped)
1 tablespoon finely shredded fresh ginger
1 tablespoon fermented black beans, coarsely chopped

SEASONING LIQUID
Combine in bowl:
3 tablespoons oyster sauce
¼ cup chicken stock
1½ teaspoons potato or cornstarch

1 large whole green onion, finely chopped *or* several fresh coriander sprigs (garnish)

1. Place mussels with about ¼ inch water in large saucepan. Cover and bring to a boil. Cook on high heat for 3 minutes, or until mussels open. Drain; discard unopened shells. When cool enough to handle, remove top of each shell and set aside.

2. Using a small, sharp knife, remove mussels from bottom of shells. Discard the bottom shells. Place mussels in small bowl; set aside. The mussels can be prepared up to this point, covered, and refrigerated until using.

3. Arrange reserved shells attractively on a heatproof platter or serving dish. Set aside.

4. Heat wok or small, heavy saucepan on high heat. Add oil; when hot, add garlic, ginger, and black beans and cook a few seconds.

5. Restir *seasoning liquid;* pour into wok. Bring to a boil, stirring, until thickened. (Sauce can be prepared a few hours ahead and refrigerated.) Set aside.

6. To serve, place platter of shells in a preheated 250° F oven for 5 minutes to heat them. Gently reheat sauce, add mussels to sauce, and heat through — only a few minutes, or they will be overcooked. Remove platter from oven; spoon mussels out of sauce onto shells. Divide sauce over mussels, making sure each one gets a few garlic slivers, ginger, and black beans. Sprinkle with green onion or coriander and serve immediately.

Serves 4.

Glazed ducks and chickens festooned on hooks, ready to be custom-chopped for the purchaser.

POULTRY

CHICKEN WITH RED-IN-SNOW

Delicate and zesty at the same time, this stir-fry gets its distinctive flavor from the preserved cabbage known as red-in-snow. I must admit this dish has the kind of earthy, unusual taste and texture combinations that I love: salty cabbage, crunchy mild-tasting bamboo shoots, earthy mushrooms, and tender chicken shreds in a delicate sauce. Red-in-snow is available in Chinese food shops and comes in small cans labeled Pickled Cabbage (not red-in-snow). Its name comes from the cabbage's red roots which sprout through the snow-covered ground in early spring. Most Chinese cookbooks say to rinse red-in-snow, but I never do because I relish its sharp taste.

2 chicken breast halves (about 1 pound), skinned, boned, and cut into matchstick-size shreds

MARINADE
Combine in bowl:
1 large egg white
2 teaspoons potato or cornstarch
1 teaspoon sugar
½ teaspoon salt
⅛ teaspoon white pepper
1 teaspoon sesame oil

7 ounce (220 g) can red-in-snow (Ma Ling brand Pickled Cabbage), drained
1 cup matchstick-size shreds bamboo shoots
7 Chinese dried black mushrooms, stems snapped off, caps soaked in hot water 30 minutes, squeezed dry, and thinly sliced
1 teaspoon sugar mixed with 2 tablespoons vegetable oil

Oil for frying
1 large garlic clove, chopped

SEASONING LIQUID
Combine in bowl:
1 tablespoon dry sherry
3 tablespoons chicken stock
1 teaspoon potato or cornstarch

1 teaspoon sesame oil

. . . .

1. Combine chicken and *marinade* in bowl; marinate for 1 hour or up to 24 hours, covered, in refrigerator.

2. Heat wok on high heat. Do not add any oil. Add red-in-snow, bamboo shoots, and mushrooms, stir-frying constantly for 30 seconds to remove excess moisture. Restir sugar and oil mixture; add to wok and stir-fry 30 seconds more. Remove vegetables to a plate.

3. Return wok to high heat. Add 1 cup oil; heat to 325°F. (The low temperature of the oil sears the chicken without browning and gives it a velvety texture.) Add chicken, stirring with chopsticks to separate shreds, and cook for about 2 minutes or until opaque. Remove and drain, leaving about 1 tablespoon oil in wok. (Clean and dry wok after draining chicken if charred bits stick to bottom, or sauce won't be clear, then add 1 tablespoon oil.)

4. Return wok to high heat. When hot, add garlic; cook a few seconds. Add cooked chicken; stir-fry a few seconds more. Return vegetables to wok; toss to mix. Restir *seasoning liquid,* pour into wok and stir to combine. Drizzle in sesame oil, toss to mix, and transfer to a heated platter.

Serves 4.

The preserved vegetable, red-in-snow, lends an exotic fragrance to the chicken in this dish.

As well as a main dish (shown above), I often serve lemon chicken as a tasty appetizer by placing the fried chicken pieces on skewers and serving the liquid seasoning in a bowl as a dipping sauce. You can also serve Sweet and Sour Chicken (page 74) this way.

WORLD'S GREATEST LEMON CHICKEN

O f the dozens of lemon chicken variations I have sampled in Chinatown over the years, there was only one that I found exceptional. The lemon sauce was nicely tart and the batter remained fairly crisp after the sauce was poured over. I begged the owner of the restaurant for the recipe but she wouldn't part with it because, of course, it was the chef's secret. So I began experimenting. It took me over a year of testing, racing back to the restaurant to compare my results, then testing again — and again — before I came up with what I think is an even superior version. The translucent sauce is lovely and tart with pretty flecks of garlic, ginger, black beans, lemon zest, and chilies showing through. But the really exciting outcome was the batter! It means the chicken can be deep-fried up to a day ahead, refrigerated, and then reheated in a 400° F oven for about 7 minutes, or until crisp, before saucing, with a result that's almost as good as freshly fried. This is terrific if you don't want to fill the air with deep-frying aromas while your guests await dinner — or if you're cooking several dishes at the same time. Just make the sauce and set aside before guests arrive, reheat batter-covered chicken on a heatproof platter in the oven, reheat sauce, and drizzle over.

2 small chicken breast halves (about ¾ pound), skinned, boned, and cut into 1-inch cubes

MARINADE
1 tablespoon water
¼ teaspoon sugar
½ teaspoon potato or cornstarch
½ teaspoon soy sauce
½ teaspoon dry sherry
½ teaspoon sesame oil

1 tablespoon vegetable oil
2 large garlic cloves, finely chopped
1 tablespoon finely chopped fresh ginger
1 teaspoon fermented black beans, coarsely chopped

Grated zest of 1 medium lemon
2 teaspoons hot bean sauce

SEASONING LIQUID
Combine in bowl:
3 tablespoons sugar
3 tablespoons fresh lemon juice
¾ cup unsweetened pineapple juice
½ teaspoon sesame oil

THICKENER
Combine in small bowl:
2 teaspoons potato starch
4 teaspoons water

BATTER
½ cup all-purpose flour
¼ cup cornstarch

(batter continued)
1 teaspoon baking powder
½ teaspoon baking soda
⅛ teaspoon salt
½ cup water
1 tablespoon hot vegetable oil

2 cups oil for deep-frying
Lemon slices or zest (optional garnish)

. . . .

1. Combine chicken and *marinade* in bowl; marinate for 1 hour or up to 24 hours, covered, in the refrigerator.

2. Heat 1 tablespoon oil in small, nonaluminum saucepan. When hot, add garlic, ginger, black beans, and grated zest. Cook, stirring, for about 30 seconds; add hot bean sauce. Stir in *seasoning liquid;* bring to a boil. Restir *thickener;* pour into sauce, stirring constantly until thickened. Sauce may be done a few hours ahead and set aside.

3. When ready to complete dish, mix *batter* dry ingredients in medium bowl. Add water; stir with chopsticks until combined but do not overmix. It will be a thick batter. Add chicken to batter; stir to mix.

4. Heat wok on high heat. Add 2 cups oil; heat to 375° F. Add 1 tablespoon of hot oil to batter; stir.

5. Using a tablespoon, spoon out batter-covered chicken pieces; deep-fry in two batches for 3 minutes or until golden brown, reheating oil to 375° F before adding next batch. Remove to a paper towel-lined plate to drain. Transfer chicken to a platter; place in preheated 400° F oven for 3 minutes — this ensures a crisp batter.

6. Meanwhile, reheat sauce, but don't let it continue to boil or it will thicken too much.

7. Drizzle sauce over chicken, garnish platter with lemon slices or top with zest if using, and serve.

Serves 4.

. . . .

SWEET AND SOUR CHICKEN

P ork is often paired with Sweet and Sour sauce, and you can substitute it or any firm white fish such as sole, halibut, or orange roughy (about 6 ounces) for the chicken in this recipe. You'll discover that this sauce is not the heavily thickened, rather cloying kind that many a Chinatown restaurant — not to mention take-out — has been known to inflict on a "Sweet and Sour" dish. I developed this recipe to satisfy my friends who are sweet and sour fans, and ended up loving it too! The right balance of sugar and vinegar plus the correct consistency makes the difference. As with Lemon Chicken (page 73), the batter-covered chicken can be deep-fried up to a day ahead, then placed in a 400° F oven for 7 minutes or until heated and crisp before adding sauce. The sauce can also be used as a dip for Deep-Fried Won Tons (page 36) or Shrimp-Stuffed Spring Rolls (page 17).

2 small chicken breast halves (about ¾ pound), skinned, boned, and cut into 1-inch cubes

MARINADE
1 tablespoon water
¼ teaspoon sugar
½ teaspoon potato or cornstarch
½ teaspoon soy sauce
½ teaspoon dry sherry
½ teaspoon sesame oil

Oil for stir-frying
2 large garlic cloves, lightly smashed with flat side of cleaver, peeled, and left whole

SEASONING LIQUID
Combine in bowl:
⅓ cup sugar
⅓ cup ketchup
⅓ cup unsweetened pineapple juice
4 tablespoons cider vinegar

THICKENER
Combine in small bowl:
2 teaspoons potato starch
4 teaspoons water

BATTER
½ cup all-purpose flour
¼ cup cornstarch
1 teaspoon baking powder
½ teaspoon baking soda
⅛ teaspoon salt
½ cup water
1 tablespoon hot vegetable oil

2 cups oil for deep-frying
1 small sweet red pepper, seeded and cut into 1-inch cubes

1. Combine chicken and *marinade* in bowl; marinate for 1 hour or up to 24 hours, covered, in refrigerator.

2. Heat 1 tablespoon oil in small nonaluminum saucepan. When hot, add garlic and cook 2 minutes or until lightly browned; remove and discard garlic. Stir in *seasoning liquid*; bring to a boil, stirring to dissolve sugar. Restir *thickener;* pour into sauce, stirring constantly until thickened. Sauce may be prepared a few hours ahead. Set aside.

3. When ready to complete dish, mix *batter* dry ingredients in a medium bowl. Add water; stir with chopsticks until combined but do not overmix. It will be a thick batter. Add chicken to batter; stir to mix.

4. Heat wok on high heat; add 2 cups oil and heat to 375° F. Add 1 tablespoon of hot oil to batter; stir.

5. Using a tablespoon, spoon out batter-covered chicken pieces, and deep-fry in two batches (reheating oil to 375° F before adding next batch) for 3 minutes or until golden brown. Remove to a paper towel-lined plate to drain, then transfer to a heated platter in a 400° F oven to crisp batter while completing dish.

6. Pour out all but 1 tablespoon oil; return wok to high heat. Add red pepper; stir-fry for 1 minute or until crisp-tender. Scoop out and arrange attractively around chicken pieces on platter.

7. Meanwhile, reheat sauce, but don't let it continue to boil or it will become too thick.

8. Drizzle sauce over chicken and serve.

Serves 4.

KUNG PAO CHICKEN

A hot and spicy dish from Szechuan province, Kung Pao Chicken (named after Ting Kung Pao who was a high-ranking Chinese official during the Ching Dynasty) is usually served in Chinatown in both Szechuan and Hunan restaurants. Chicken thigh meat is ideal here because it has the right textural quality. For years I tried to find the secret marinade that would give the distinctive texture of stir-fried chicken as served in Chinese restaurants — slightly slippery and "smooth". It wasn't until I accidentally thawed some chicken thighs instead of breasts one day, that I discovered the secret ingredient wasn't the marinade at all! Boning chicken thighs (see Glossary for instructions) isn't too difficult once you get the hang of it, though a sharp knife is absolutely essential. You can use breast meat if you wish, but the texture won't be quite the same.

6 chicken thighs or 2 breast halves, (1½ pounds) skinned, boned, and cut into ½-inch cubes

MARINADE
2 tablespoons water
1 teaspoon soy sauce
1 tablespoon potato or cornstarch
1 teaspoon sesame oil

Vegetable oil for stir-frying
2 large garlic cloves, chopped
20 dried red chilies (left whole for mild, 10 broken in half for hot, all broken in half for very hot)
4 large whole green onions, chopped

SEASONING LIQUID
Combine in bowl:
2 tablespoons soy sauce

(seasoning liquid continued)
2 tablespoons red wine vinegar
1 tablespoon dry sherry
2 teaspoons sugar
1 tablespoon chili oil
1 teaspoon potato or cornstarch
¼ teaspoon salt

1 tablespoon sesame oil
½ cup salted peanuts

. . . .

1. Combine chicken and *marinade* in bowl; marinate 2 hours or up to 24 hours, covered, in refrigerator.

2. Heat wok on high heat. Add 3 tablespoons oil; when hot, add chicken and stir-fry for 2 to 3 minutes or until opaque. Remove to a strainer to drain excess oil. Clean and dry wok if charred bits stick to bottom.

3. Return to high heat; add 1 tablespoon oil. When hot, add garlic, chilies (including seeds), and green onions. Stir-fry for 30 seconds or until chilies begin to blacken. Return chicken to wok, restir *seasoning liquid,* and pour over chicken. Toss for 30 seconds or until glazed with sauce. Drizzle in sesame oil, add peanuts, and stir. Transfer to a heated platter.

Serves 2 to 4.

BRAISED ORANGE CHICKEN

Braising chicken in a sauce with the wonderful flavors of orange zest, garlic, ginger, chili paste, and hoisin sauce creates very tender, luscious meat in a rich, savory broth. This dish has the advantage that it can be prepared ahead of time and gently reheated. I chop the chicken legs using a very heavy cleaver with the aid of a rubber mallet. Lacking these implements, ask your butcher to chop them for you. Before cooking, check for and remove from the cut areas of the chicken, any loose and shattered bones. You can do half chicken legs and half breasts, but my personal preference is legs only. Don't try this dish with boneless chicken. The bones flavor the stock and the chicken requires the longer cooking time to achieve the right texture.

2 tablespoons vegetable oil
4 chicken legs (about 2 pounds),
  skinned and each chopped into
  4 pieces
4 large garlic cloves, left whole,
  lightly smashed with flat side
  of cleaver, and peeled
1-inch piece of fresh ginger, smashed
  with flat side of cleaver
1 medium onion, cut into wedges
  (eighths) and separated
Grated zest of 1 large orange
1 teaspoon chili paste with soy bean

BRAISING LIQUID
2 tablespoons soy sauce
2 tablespoons dry sherry
1 tablespoon hoisin sauce
¼ cup chicken stock

THICKENER
Combine in small bowl:
2 teaspoons potato or cornstarch
2 teaspoons water

1 teaspoon sesame oil
Fresh coriander sprigs (garnish)

· · · · · · · · · · ·

1. Heat oil in large nonstick or heavy skillet Add chicken; cook until golden brown on all sides. Add garlic, ginger, onion, orange zest, and chili paste; cook another 2 minutes.

2. Transfer chicken and seasonings to heavy medium saucepan (leaving behind excess oil if any).

3. Pour *braising liquid* over chicken. Bring to a boil on high heat, cover, and reduce heat to medium-low. Simmer gently for 1 hour, lifting lid occasionally to stir, until chicken is very tender.

4. Restir *thickener,* pour into saucepan; stir until thickened. Drizzle in sesame oil, stir, and transfer to a serving dish. Garnish with coriander.

Serves 2 to 4.

PAPER WRAPPED CHICKEN

Always a delight to guests when they open the paper packages at the table to find tender, fragrant pieces of chicken, mushrooms, and green onion or coriander inside, these little parcels make a wonderful first course or a main dish, if served with other dishes. The paper parcels are made up of either parchment or heavy cellophane paper, they are filled, then deep-fried in hot oil. They can be prepared several hours ahead and refrigerated before frying. To eat, the parcels are opened either with chopsticks (very tricky!) or with the fingers, and then the filling is eaten with chopsticks. Provide plenty of napkins and a bowl for discarding paper.

2 chicken breast halves, (about 1½ pounds), skinned, boned, each cut in half lengthwise, and thinly sliced on the diagonal

MARINADE
1 tablespoon soy sauce
1 tablespoon dry sherry
1 tablespoon sesame oil
2 teaspoons hoisin sauce
1 large garlic clove, finely chopped
1 tablespoon finely chopped fresh ginger

Approximately 26 6 x 6-inch pieces parchment or heavy cellophane paper
Sesame oil for brushing parchment paper
Fresh coriander sprigs and/or 6 large green onions (green part only), cut into 2-inch pieces
6 Chinese dried black mushrooms, stems snapped off, caps soaked for 30 minutes in hot water, squeezed dry, and thinly sliced
Oil for deep-frying

1. Combine chicken and *marinade* in bowl; marinate for about 30 minutes, not too much longer or flavor will be too strong.

2. Fold all the pieces of paper in half to make a rectangle, then unfold, and stack. Take one piece of paper; brush inside very lightly with sesame oil.

3. Place 1 piece chicken (leaving behind marinade), 1 coriander sprig or 2 pieces green onion, and 1 piece mushroom in the center of one half of the oiled side.

4. Fold over other half of paper. Starting with the long side, fold each open edge over twice, about ¼ inch each fold, to seal edges. Press and pinch edges to seal securely. If seal isn't tight, the parcels will open while they are being fried. Continue until all pieces of paper are filled. A second way to fold paper is candywrapper-style (only with

cellophane): fold the long edge as described above, then carefully crimp and twist each end to seal, being very careful not to tear paper.

5. Heat wok on high heat. Add 4 cups oil; heat to 350° F. Drop in several packages; deep-fry (they actually float on top of the oil) for about 30 seconds, then turn over and cook another 30 seconds or until chicken is cooked through. Remove with tongs — holding them up for a few seconds over wok to allow excess oil to drip off — to a paper towel-lined plate to drain. Open one to check doneness and continue until all are done. Pile parcels on top of one another on a serving dish.

Makes about 26 parcels.

Tender morsels of chicken and vegetables tucked inside a cellophane envelope make a special main dish or starter.

CHICKEN WITH THREE MUSHROOMS

T he Chinese name for this dish is Moo Goo Gai Pan — goo is the word for mushroom; moo goo means button mushroom; gai means chicken, and pan means slices. When I first began developing this recipe I thought using fresh mushrooms in place of the ever-present canned button mushrooms would no doubt bring this dish to new heights. I was wrong. Ordinary canned button mushrooms are essential to the "authenticity" of this Chinatown classic. When cooked alongside dried Chinese mushrooms and the brown umbrella-shaped straw mushrooms, they combine to make a delicious dish with a distinctive mushroom flavor. Straw mushrooms are available canned or dried. The canned variety are used here. They look attractive and have a pleasant slippery texture that makes it great fun to watch even seasoned chopstick users — including my Chinese friends — attempt to pick them up without dropping them! It's easier to slice the chicken paper-thin if it's slightly frozen.

2 small chicken breast halves
  (¾ pound), skinned, boned, cut in
  half lengthwise, then thinly sliced
  on the diagonal

MARINADE
1 tablespoon water
⅛ teaspoon salt
1 teaspoon potato or cornstarch

Oil for stir-frying
1 large garlic clove, chopped
1 tablespoon finely chopped
  fresh ginger
6 Chinese dried black mushrooms,
  stems snapped off, caps soaked for
  30 minutes in hot water,
  squeezed dry, and thinly sliced
6 canned baby corn, cut in half
  lengthwise
6 snow peas, ends trimmed
½ cup canned whole button
  mushrooms
½ cup canned whole straw
  mushrooms

SEASONING LIQUID
Combine in bowl:
1 tablespoon oyster sauce
1 tablespoon dry sherry
1 teaspoon soy sauce
¼ teaspoon salt
¼ teaspoon sugar
⅓ cup chicken stock

THICKENER
Combine in small bowl:
2 teaspoons potato or cornstarch
1 tablespoon water

· · · · · · · · · · ·

1. Combine chicken and *marinade* in bowl; marinate 2 hours or up to 24 hours, covered, in refrigerator.

2. Heat wok on high heat. Add 2 tablespoons oil; when hot, add chicken and stir-fry for 2 to 3 minutes or until opaque. Remove to a plate.

Clean and dry wok if charred bits stick to bottom.

3. Return to high heat; add another tablespoon oil, then add garlic, ginger, Chinese mushrooms, and baby corn. Toss for about 30 seconds; add snow peas, remaining mushrooms, and cooked chicken. Stir-fry for 30 seconds or until chicken is heated through.

4. Stir in *seasoning liquid*; bring to a boil. Restir *thickener*; pour into wok, stir until thickened, and transfer to a heated platter.

Serves 4

SZECHUAN CRISPY DUCK

D uck is superb cooked by this method: first steamed to render out most of the fat, then deep-fried to crisp the skin. Though not traditional, I have devised a "Chinese cole slaw" to serve with this dish that counterbalances the duck beautifully. Don't make the salad too far in advance: you must preserve the fresh flavor and crispness of the cabbage (I make it just before I begin deep-frying, though it can be prepared up to an hour ahead. You can serve the salad as a vegetable with other main dishes, too.)

1 whole duck (4½ to 5 pounds), thawed if frozen
2 tablespoons dry sherry
2 tablespoons five spice powder
½ cup cornstarch

1½ pounds white cabbage, cored and shredded using the slicing disk, not the shredding disk of a food processor

DRESSING
1½ tablespoons sugar
2 tablespoons rice vinegar
2 tablespoons sesame oil
1 teaspoon salt

8 cups vegetable oil for deep-frying
Spicy salt for dipping (optional)

1. Remove fat from cavity and neck of duck. Rinse under cold running water, drain, and dry thoroughly with paper towels.

2. Rub dry sherry over skin and inside cavity. Set aside for 5 minutes, then pat dry with paper towels.

3. Rub five spice powder evenly over skin and inside cavity. Place duck inside a large freezer bag; close with a twist tie or wrap in plastic wrap and place in a bowl. Refrigerate for several hours, preferably overnight.

5. Remove duck from plastic bag or wrap; place on a heatproof dish (a Pyrex pie plate works well).

6. Place a rack in wok; fill with water to bottom edge of rack. Cover; bring to a boil. Place duck in dish over boiling water, cover, and steam for 2 hours. (Check water level every ½ hour; replenish with hot water when necessary. Pour off accumulated fat and liquid if dish becomes full.)

7. Remove duck from wok; allow to air-dry on a rack for 1 hour. (At this point the duck can be covered and refrigerated several hours. Bring back to room temperature before frying.)

8. Rub cornstarch all over the outside of duck, pressing lightly to make it adhere.

9. Mix cabbage with *dressing* in a large bowl, cover, and refrigerate.

10. In a clean, dry wok, heat oil to 400° F. Carefully lower duck, breast side down, into oil; deep-fry for about 8 to 10 minutes, continually ladling oil over exposed part of duck, until skin is crisp and browned. Remove; drain duck on a paper towel-lined plate, then chop through the bones into bite-size pieces. Arrange on a large platter edged with cole slaw or serve salad in a separate bowl. Serve with spicy salt.

Serves 4 to 6.

Fast food Chinese-style at a barbecue shop.

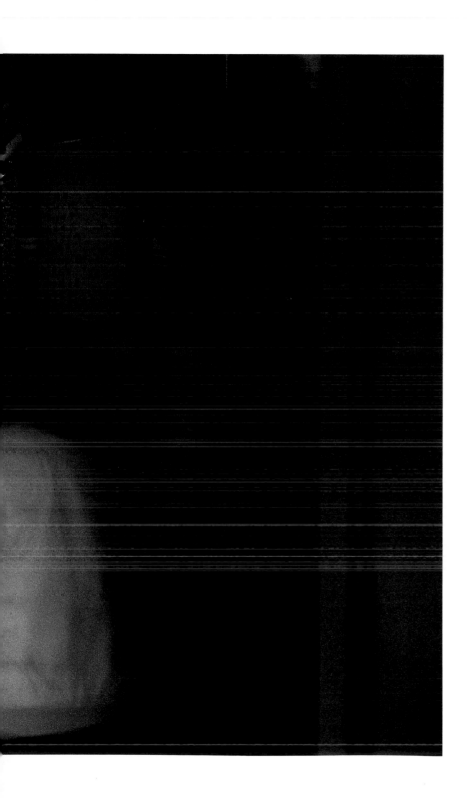

PORK

PEARL BALLS

Not every Hunan dish is spicy hot. These delicate meatballs rolled in pearly sweet (glutinous) rice and gently steamed are one such. Once steamed, the glutinous rice coating becomes beautifully translucent and shining — the color of pearls, hence the name. The rice is soaked first, to soften before steaming, and once the meatballs are coated with it, they must be steamed right away or the rice will dry out. They can be prepared and steamed ahead, then resteamed once more without too much loss of flavor.

1 pound ground pork
1 egg
6 Chinese dried black mushrooms, stems snapped off, caps soaked for 30 minutes in hot water, squeezed dry, and diced
2 whole green onions, finely chopped
6 fresh or canned water chestnuts, chopped

SEASONINGS
1 tablespoon sugar
1 tablespoon soy sauce
1 tablespoon dry sherry
1 tablespoon sesame oil
½ teaspoon salt

1 cup sweet rice, rinsed well, soaked for 4 hours in cold water to cover

GARLIC SOY DIP
Combine in small bowl:
2 tablespoons soy sauce
1 tablespoon red wine vinegar
1 teaspoon sesame oil
¼ teaspoon sugar
1 small garlic clove, finely chopped

1. Combine pork, egg, mushrooms, green onions, water chestnuts, and *seasonings*.

2. Drain rice; spread out on a tray.

3. Form pork mixture into meat balls, using about a heaping tablespoonful for each. Roll pork balls over rice, making sure they are completely covered. Place them on a lightly oiled, heatproof dish (I use a Pyrex pie plate), about ½ inch apart. (The pork balls will not all fit on one plate, so you will have to steam them in about 3 batches.)

4. Place a rack in wok; fill wok with water to bottom edge of rack. Cover; bring to a boil.

5. Place dish containing pork balls on rack, cover, and steam for 15 minutes on high heat or until they are cooked through and rice turns shiny and translucent. Do not

overcook. Cook remaining pork balls in the same manner.

6. Remove to a heated serving platter and serve with Garlic Soy Dip.

Serves 4 to 6.

MA PO PORK AND BEAN CURD

According to legend this highly spiced dish was created in the Ching Dynasty by one Chen Ma Po, the pock-marked wife of the owner of a small eatery in the city of Chengtu, capital of Szechuan province. Even if uncomplimentary, the Chinese find humor in nicknaming people because of their physical appearance. That is why this dish became famous in China as Pock-Marked Old Woman or Bean Curd of the Pock-Marked Wife. If you see it so named on Chinatown menus, don't be put off. You wouldn't want to miss this hot and spicy bean curd dish exploding with flavor! Since it can be made ahead and reheated gently in the oven — without any last minute flurry — it makes a splendid dish to serve alongside a stir-fried dish plus an appetizer and soup for a dinner party.

2 to 3 tablespoons oil for frying
4 large garlic cloves, finely chopped
2 tablespoons finely chopped fresh ginger
3 tablespoons coarsely diced Szechuan preserved vegetable
10 ounces ground pork
4 cakes bean curd (1 pound), drained and cut into 1-inch cubes

SEASONING LIQUID
Combine in bowl:
3 tablespoons hot bean sauce
1 tablespoon soy sauce
1 teaspoon mushroom soy sauce
1 teaspoon sugar

THICKENER
Combine in small bowl:
1 tablespoon potato or cornstarch
2 tablespoons water

1 teaspoon sesame oil
2 whole green onions, finely chopped

1. Heat wok on high heat. Add oil; when hot, add garlic, ginger, and Szechuan vegetable. Stir-fry, tossing constantly over high heat for a few seconds. Add pork; stir-fry, breaking up any lumps, until no pink remains. Tilt wok; scoop out excess oil, if necessary.

2. Add bean curd; toss gently. Cover; cook 2 minutes. Remove lid; add *seasoning liquid* and toss to mix.

3. Restir *thickener;* add to wok. Drizzle in sesame oil, stir, then sprinkle in green onions.

Serves 4 to 6.

Shredded Pork in Hoisin Sauce. This dish can also be served with an additional border of deep-fried rice stick noodles, then spoonfuls of the pork, green onion shreds, and noodles are wrapped in lettuce leaves and eaten with the fingers.

SHREDDED PORK IN HOISIN SAUCE

R ich sauced pork served on a bed of shredded green onions makes an exuberant, pretty presentation. I've added shredded bamboo shoots for color and crunch and to help cut both the sweetness and the richness of the sauce. This Northern Chinese dish is easy to prepare and is often served with steamed Mandarin Pancakes (page 27) although it's just as enjoyable without.

¾ pound pork tenderloin, cut into matchstick-size shreds

MARINADE
3 tablespoons water
2 teaspoons soy sauce
1 teaspoon dry sherry
½ teaspoon sesame oil
2 teaspoons potato or cornstarch

6 whole green onions, shredded
2 cups vegetable oil for deep-frying

SEASONING LIQUID
Combine in bowl:
3 tablespoons hoisin sauce
1 tablespoon dry sherry
1 tablespoon soy sauce
1 tablespoon sugar

½ cup matchstick-size shreds bamboo shoots

1. Combine pork and *marinade* in bowl; marinate for 1 hour or up to 24 hours, covered, in refrigerator.

2. Attractively arrange green onions in a layer on a serving dish. Set aside.

3. Heat wok on high heat. Add oil; heat to 375°F. Add pork; deep-fry, stirring with chopsticks to break up shreds, for about 3 to 4 minutes or until no pink remains, then drain.

4. Return wok to high heat. Add pork and *seasoning liquid* to wok; toss for 1 minute or until pork absorbs sauce and is heated through. Toss in bamboo shoots, mix swiftly, then scoop out and place mixture in center of green onions.

Serves 2 to 4.

SPARERIBS IN CHEF'S SPECIAL SAUCE

Succulent ribs, double-fried (first deep-fried, then stir-fried) in a slightly sweet and savory sauce, are a well-established dish in many a Chinatown chef's repertoire. I have used the double-frying technique in developing many other recipes too — not always Chinese ones — because the first frying in oil crisps while the second frying forces the sauce to cling and be absorbed into the food, thus creating a very intensely flavored morsel. Ask the butcher to slice between each rib, then slice each bone in half crosswise with his electric saw, if you don't have a heavy cleaver.

1½ pounds meaty spareribs, sliced between each rib, chopped in half crosswise through the bone with heavy cleaver, loose bone fragments removed

MARINADE
1 tablespoon soy sauce
1 tablespoon dry sherry
1 large garlic clove, minced
1 tablespoon sugar
½ teaspoon salt

1 egg, beaten
1 cup cornstarch, on piece of wax paper

4 cups oil for deep frying

SEASONING LIQUID
Combine in bowl:
2 tablespoons Worcestershire sauce
3 tablespoons water
3 tablespoons ketchup
1 teaspoon sugar
½ teaspoon sesame oil

1. Combine spareribs and *marinade* in large bowl; marinate 2 hours or up to 24 hours, covered, in refrigerator.

2. Dip marinated ribs in beaten egg; roll in cornstarch to coat evenly. At this point the ribs can be refrigerated and covered with plastic wrap for several hours. Bring back to room temperature before deep-frying.

3. Heat wok on high heat. Add oil; heat to 380° F. Deep-fry ribs in 2 batches (reheating oil to 380°F before adding 2nd batch) for about 3 to 5 minutes or until golden brown and cooked through. Remove ribs to a paper towel-lined plate to drain.

4. Drain all but 1 tablespoon oil from wok; return to high heat. Add ribs and *seasoning liquid;* toss to coat ribs. Continue tossing for about 30 seconds, then remove to a heated platter. The ribs can be placed in a 250°F oven for a few minutes to keep warm if you are preparing other dishes at the same time.

Serves 4 to 6.

Bite-size, sweet-and-savory-sauced ribs served with ice-cold Chinese beer.

STIR-FRIED PORK IN FRAGRANT SAUCE

S uffused with delicately spicy seasonings of Szechuan origin, the shredded pork and crunchy vegetables are tasty and subtly hot. In Chinese, this dish is called Pork in Fish-Flavored Sauce, but I've taken the liberty of giving it a more appealing name. No fish is used to flavor the dish — rather, this sauce traditionally goes with fish.

½ pound pork tenderloin, sliced into matchstick-size shreds

MARINADE
1½ teaspoons soy sauce
½ teaspoon dry sherry
1 teaspoon sesame oil
1 teaspoon potato or cornstarch

Oil for stir-frying
3 large garlic cloves, chopped
1 tablespoon finely chopped fresh ginger
4 medium tree ears, soaked for 20 minutes in hot water, knobby parts cut off, and sliced into julienne
1 medium stalk celery, sliced into julienne
2 whole green onions, chopped

SEASONING LIQUID
Combine in bowl:
1 tablespoon sugar
1½ tablespoons soy sauce

(seasoning liquid continued)
1 tablespoon dry sherry
1 tablespoon red wine vinegar
1 tablespoon chili paste with soy bean

THICKENER
Combine in small bowl:
1 teaspoon potato or cornstarch
1 tablespoon water

2 teaspoons sesame oil

. . . .

1. Combine pork and *marinade* in bowl; marinate for 30 minutes or up to 24 hours, covered, in refrigerator.

2. Heat wok on high heat. Add 2 tablespoons oil; when hot, add pork. Stir-fry for 3 minutes or until pork is no longer pink; remove to a plate.

3. Add more oil if necessary, then garlic, ginger, tree ears, and celery; toss for 2 minutes or until celery is crisp-tender.

4. Return pork to wok, then add green onions. Pour in *seasoning liquid;* toss until sauce is bubbling. Restir *thickener,* pour into wok, and stir-fry for 1 minute to thicken and allow pork to absorb flavors. Drizzle in sesame oil, toss, and transfer mixture to a heated platter.

Serves 2 to 4.

CHINESE BARBECUED PORK

T he Chinese very seldom make their own barbecued pork (char siu), instead, they buy it in specialty stores where it's sold by weight. Barbecued pork is eaten as a snack, appetizer, or with rice or noodle dishes, stir-fries, or used in fillings for dim sum. I like to make my own barbecued pork because the Chinatown version is made with pork butt which is fattier than pork tenderloin. For more authenticity you can substitute boneless pork butt if you wish.

2 pork tenderloins (about ¾ pound each)

MARINADE
¼ cup sugar
¼ cup soy sauce
¼ cup dry sherry
¼ cup hoisin sauce
¼ cup ketchup
4 large garlic cloves, lightly smashed with flat side of cleaver, and peeled
1 tablespoon finely chopped fresh ginger
½ teaspoon five spice powder

GLAZE
Combine in small bowl:
3 tablespoons honey
1 tablespoon boiling water
1 tablespoon red wine vinegar
1 tablespoon sesame oil

1. Place pork tenderloins and *marinade* in medium bowl. Turn pork several times to coat thoroughly with marinade; leave at room temperature for 30 minutes, turning every 10 minutes or so. Cover, and refrigerate overnight, turning occasionally.

2. Add about 1 cup water to bottom of broiling pan. Remove pork from marinade; place on rack, then on top of pan containing water.

3. Place broiling pan with pork in preheated 400° F oven; bake 20 minutes, basting every 10 minutes with marinade, then reduce heat to 350° F and cook another 25 minutes or until pork is cooked and no longer pink in center. Baste pork with *glaze* during last 10 minutes of baking.

4. Remove pork from oven and allow to cool to room temperature before using. It is now ready for use in other dishes and can be refrigerated for 2 to 3 days or serve at room temperature, thinly sliced, and arranged on a serving platter with plum sauce or Chinese mustard (see Glossary).

Serves 4 to 6.

The wonderful combination of flavors and textures makes this an attractive party dish.

MU SHU PORK

Enormously popular in Chinatown restaurants, this Northern Chinese dish is usually served with Mandarin Pancakes, into which the filling is wrapped. The pancakes can be made and the meat and vegetables prepared and chopped up to a day ahead, leaving only a quick stir-fry and steaming at the last minute. Try substituting chicken or beef for the pork or omitting the meat altogether for a vegetarian version. The sweet red and yellow peppers are my addition: it's not classic, but I think it gives the dish more eye appeal and piquancy. Serve with Chicken with Fresh Tomato and Ginger Soup (page 39) for a simple dinner.

¼ pound pork tenderloin, cut into matchstick-size shreds

MARINADE
¼ teaspoon salt
¼ teaspoon sugar
⅛ teaspoon white pepper
1½ teaspoons water
1 teaspoon soy sauce
½ teaspoon dry sherry
1 teaspoon potato or cornstarch

Oil for stir-frying
3 eggs, well beaten with ½ teaspoon sesame oil
Mandarin Pancakes (see page 27)
2 large garlic cloves, chopped
1 tablespoon finely chopped fresh ginger
½ cup dried lily buds, soaked in cold water for 20 minutes, squeezed dry, hard parts cut off
3 small tree ears, soaked in hot water for 20 minutes, knobby parts cut off, sliced into thin julienne
6 Chinese dried black mushrooms, stems snapped off, caps soaked for 30 minutes in hot water, squeezed dry, thinly sliced
½ cup julienned sweet red pepper, or a combination of yellow and red peppers

½ cup shredded bamboo shoots
2 large whole green onions, shredded
2 tablespoons soy sauce
2 tablespoons dry sherry
1 tablespoon sesame oil
Hoisin sauce for spreading
Green onion brushes (see Glossary)

· · · · · · · · · ·

1. Combine pork and *marinade* in bowl; marinate for 1 hour or up to 24 hours, covered, in refrigerator.

2. Heat 2 teaspoons oil in wok. Pour in eggs; tilt pan to distribute into a thin pancake. Cook for 2 minutes or until set – no need to flip over. Remove to a plate; when cool enough to handle, cut into julienne. Set aside.

3. When ready to begin, steam pancakes by placing on a rack over boiling water in a wok or steamer. Cover; steam 5 minutes. Leave cover on wok until ready to serve. (Do not heat pancakes in oven or they will be too dry.)

4. Heat a second wok or a large nonstick skillet on high heat. Add 2 tablespoons oil; when hot, add pork. Stir-fry for 1 to 2 minutes or until no longer pink. Add garlic and ginger; toss. Add lily buds, tree ears, and mushrooms; toss 30 seconds. Add more oil if necessary, then sweet pepper and bamboo shoots; toss a few seconds. Add green onions, then soy sauce, dry sherry, and sesame oil, tossing to combine. Toss in egg shreds. Transfer to a heated platter. Place pancakes folded in either halves or quarters around edge of platter or on separate serving dish.

5. To eat, each person spreads pancake with hoisin sauce using green onion brushes, then places some pork mixture on pancake, folds it over, and eats sandwich style.

Serves 4 to 6.

A mirror image of the colorful, hand-lettered signs that decorate this popular lunch spot.

BEEF

GINGER BEEF

Q uick to cook, yet full of flavor, this dish combines beef with a generous amount of ginger shreds that are first salted, then rinsed to soften the hotness of the ginger. If you come across "young" or "baby" ginger with its thin cream-colored skin and pink-tipped shoots (available only during early summer to early fall), by all means substitute it for the "older" ginger. Because it has a milder taste, the "young" ginger doesn't need presalting.

½ pound flank steak, thinly sliced against the grain

MARINADE
1 large egg white
1 tablespoon soy sauce
1 tablespoon potato or cornstarch
⅛ teaspoon white pepper
1 teaspoon sesame oil

2 tablespoons vegetable oil
½ cup julienned fresh ginger, tossed with 1 teaspoon salt, rinsed after 10 minutes, patted dry with paper towels
4 large whole green onions, shredded (if not using coriander)
1 cup chopped fresh coriander (if not using green onions)

SEASONING LIQUID
Combine in bowl:
2 tablespoons oyster sauce
1 tablespoon water
1 teaspoon sugar
1 teaspoon soy sauce
1 teaspoon dry sherry
1 teaspoon sesame oil
¼ teaspoon potato or cornstarch

. . . .

1. Combine beef and *marinade* in bowl; marinate for 2 hours or up to 24 hours, covered, in refrigerator.

2. Heat wok on high heat. Add oil; when hot, add beef and stir-fry for 30 seconds or until beef is browned but still slightly rare. Remove to a plate.

3. Add another tablespoon oil if necessary; add ginger and green onions (if using), then toss for 30 seconds. Return beef to wok and stir-fry for 30 seconds or until heated through. Add coriander (if using), then restir *seasoning liquid* and pour into wok. Stir until thickened and serve.

Serves 4.

BEEF CHOW FUN IN BLACK BEAN SAUCE

Beef and fresh rice flour noodles stir-fried, then combined with a savory sauce heightened by pungent fermented black beans creates a rich, comforting dish. Slippery-textured, fresh rice noodles (sa fun) are available in clear plastic bags in Chinatown food stores in the fresh noodle section. Although they appear to be one solid white hunk of noodle, they are actually tightly packed noodle ribbons that must be separated gently before cooking. (But also note that there are uncut rice flour noodle wrappers available in the fresh noodle section. Check to be sure they are cut into ribbons.) When purchasing, look at the noodles carefully. They should be very moist and oily-looking to guarantee freshness.

½ pound flank steak, thinly sliced against the grain

MARINADE
1 teaspoon soy sauce
1 teaspoon dry sherry
¼ teaspoon sugar
1 teaspoon cornstarch
1½ teaspoons vegetable oil

Oil for stir-frying
1 medium onion, cut into wedges (sixteenths)
2 large garlic cloves, chopped
1 tablespoon finely chopped fresh ginger
3 whole green onions, finely chopped
1 tablespoon fermented black beans, coarsely chopped
¾ pound fresh rice noodles (sa fun), separated

SEASONING LIQUID
Combine in bowl:
⅓ cup chicken stock

(seasoning liquid continued)
3 tablespoons water
1 tablespoon oyster sauce
1 teaspoon soy sauce
1½ teaspoons potato or cornstarch

. . . .

1. Combine beef and *marinade* (stirring in first 4 ingredients before adding oil) in bowl; marinate for 2 hours or up to 24 hours, covered, in refrigerator.

2. Heat wok on high heat. Add 2 tablespoons oil; when hot, add onion and toss for 1 minute or until translucent. Remove to a plate; set aside.

3. Add a little more oil if necessary; add garlic, ginger, green onions, and black beans. Cook a few seconds; add beef. Stir-fry for 1 minute or until browned but still slightly rare.

Remove; set mixture aside with onion.

4. Add another 2 tablespoons oil. Add rice noodles; stir-fry gently for about 2 minutes. Try to prevent noodles from sticking too much, adding more oil if necessary. But don't worry if they scorch a little: any crusty bits on the noodles will improve their flavor.

5. Return cooked ingredients to wok; toss to distribute. Restir *seasoning liquid;* pour into wok and toss until thickened. Transfer to a heated platter.

Serves 4.

Here crisp and chewy "dry-fried" beef is shown sans sauce. This piquant dish tastes spicy hot, sweet, and savory all at once.

SZECHUAN DRY-FRIED BEEF WITH VEGETABLES

G reat patience was needed to prepare this famous, deliciously spicy dish in the traditional way: the beef was sautéed for up to an hour on low heat until very dry and crisp. Today the beef is deep-fried until crisp, then stir-fried with seasonings to create a similar texture in only minutes. The beef can be deep-fried several hours ahead, covered, refrigerated, and brought back to room temperature before completing dish.

½ pound flank steak, cut into matchstick-size shreds

MARINADE
1 tablespoon soy sauce
1 tablespoon dry sherry
2 teaspoons sugar
1 tablespoon finely chopped fresh ginger

⅓ cup cornstarch
Oil for deep-frying
2 large garlic cloves, chopped
1 tablespoon finely chopped fresh ginger
1 large stalk celery, leaves removed and cut into julienne
2 medium carrots, cut into julienne
1 large whole green onion, shredded

SEASONING LIQUID
Combine in bowl:
2½ tablespoons soy sauce
2 tablespoons water
1½ teaspoons sugar
1½ teaspoons red wine vinegar
1½ teaspoons chili paste with soy bean
2 teaspoons sesame oil
½ teaspoon potato or cornstarch

1. Combine beef and *marinade* in bowl; marinate for 30 minutes or up to 24 hours, covered, in refrigerator.

2. Place cornstarch on a piece of wax paper; coat beef shreds completely.

3. Heat wok on high heat. Add 2 cups oil; heat to 375° F. Deep-fry beef in 4 batches, for 1 minute each or until browned and crisp. Remove beef shreds with a Chinese strainer or slotted spoon to a paper towel-lined plate to drain.

4. Pour out all but 1 tablespoon oil; return wok to high heat. Add garlic and ginger; cook a few seconds. Add vegetables, then add 1 tablespoon water to wok. Immediately cover; steam-cook for 1 minute. Remove lid; if any liquid remains, cook until completely evaporated.

5. Return beef to wok; toss 30 seconds to heat through. Restir

seasoning liquid; pour into wok. Stir until glazed. Transfer to a heated serving dish.

Serves 2 to 4.

CHINESE BEEF STEW

We first tasted a lamb stew when some Chinese friends ordered it for us in Chinatown. Most non-Chinese are very familiar with stir-fried and steamed dishes in Chinese cooking, but don't realize that stewed and braised dishes are also an ancient and authentic part of Chinese cuisine. The following recipe is my own creation, based on a combination of the lamb stew I enjoyed so much in Chinatown and a traditional Chinese beef stew. The pungent, rich gravy is delicious over rice, the beef is incredibly tender and flavorful, the softened bean curd sticks absorb the earthy flavors, while the carrots and the fresh water chestnuts or Chinese turnip (daikon radish) add crispness and color. As with most stews, it tastes even better when reheated the following day. This stew needs no accompaniment other than White Rice (page 44) and perhaps Fermented Bean Curd Dip (page 101, caption) or Stir-Fried Spinach with Fermented Bean Curd (page 108). Since it can be done in advance, remember that it's also perfect for serving with other dishes as part of a multicourse meal.

6 9-inch dried bean curd sticks, broken into 4 pieces
2¾ pounds beef brisket or stewing beef, trimmed and cut into 1½-inch cubes
6 large garlic cloves, peeled and left whole
6 slices fresh ginger
4 pieces dried tangerine peel (each about 3 inches long)
3 whole star anise
1 medium onion, quartered
Oil for stir-frying

SEASONING LIQUID
½ cup soy sauce
2 cups water
¼ cup dry sherry
2 tablespoons sugar
1 teaspoon salt

8 to 10 medium carrots, roll cut (see Glossary)
8 peeled, fresh water chestnuts or ½ pound Chinese turnip (daikon radish), cut into the same size as carrots

THICKENER
Combine in small bowl:
3 tablespoons potato or cornstarch
3 tablespoons water

Fresh coriander sprigs (garnish)

• • • • • • • • • •

1. Cover bean curd sticks with warm water in medium bowl. Set aside for 2 hours. (They will be softened and ready to add to the stew when the beef is tender.)

2. Place beef, garlic, ginger, tangerine peel, star anise, and onion on a plate and set beside wok or large (12-inch) nonstick skillet.

3. Heat wok or skillet on high heat. Add 3 tablespoons oil; when hot, stir-fry beef, garlic, ginger, tangerine peel, star anise, and onion in several batches until beef is browned, adding more oil if necessary. (Do not overcrowd wok or skillet; this will steam-cook the beef instead of browning it nicely.) Remove each batch to a heavy 5-quart saucepan.

4. Add *seasoning liquid* to the saucepan. Stir to mix with the beef; bring to a boil. Reduce heat to low; simmer, covered, 2 hours or until meat is tender.

5. Drain bean curd sticks; squeeze out excess moisture. Add these, plus carrots and fresh water chestnuts or turnip to saucepan. Stir, cover, and continue cooking for 1 more hour.

6. Restir *thickener;* add to saucepan. Stir until thickened. Transfer to a serving bowl; garnish with several coriander sprigs.

Serves 6.

Warming to the body and pleasing to the palate, this dark, comforting stew is a favorite for autumn and winter entertaining. The stew is served with a small dish of fermented bean curd dip. To make, mix 1 cube fermented bean curd with about 1 teaspoon of its liquid, and 1 teaspoon sesame oil until just combined.

BEEF AND BROCCOLI

A lighter approach to Beef and Broccoli, this is not the typical restaurant version which often combines them in a thick, cornstarched sauce. Here, the broccoli and sweet red pepper are cooked separately, with the beef and sauce served atop, happily retaining the distinctive flavors and brilliant colors of each ingredient.

½ pound flank steak, thinly sliced
  against the grain

MARINADE
1 large egg white
1 tablespoon soy sauce
1 tablespoon potato or cornstarch
⅛ teaspoon white pepper
½ teaspoon sesame oil

Oil for stir-frying
1 large garlic clove, chopped
1 tablespoon finely chopped fresh
  ginger
¼ pound broccoli florets (not stems),
  cut into bite-size pieces, (about
  2 cups)
1 medium onion, cut into wedges
  (eighths)
½ sweet red pepper, seeded and
  cubed
⅛ teaspoon sugar
⅛ teaspoon salt
3 tablespoons water

SEASONING LIQUID
Combine in bowl:
5 tablespoons chicken stock
3 tablespoons oyster sauce
1 tablespoon dry sherry
2 teaspoons soy sauce
½ teaspoon sugar
1 teaspoon potato or cornstarch

. . . .

1. Combine beef and *marinade* in bowl; marinate for 2 hours or up to 24 hours, covered, in refrigerator.

2. Heat wok on high heat. Add 2 tablespoons oil; when hot, add garlic, ginger, broccoli, onion, and red pepper. Sprinkle with sugar and salt; toss for 1 minute. Add water, immediately cover, and steam-cook for 2 minutes or until broccoli is tender-crisp and still bright green. Remove to a heated platter. Keep warm.

3. Clean and dry wok; return to high heat. Add 3 tablespoons oil; when hot, add beef. Stir-fry for 1 minute or until beef is medium rare. Restir *seasoning liquid,* pour into wok, and toss until thickened. Immediately scoop out and spoon over broccoli.

Serves 2 to 4.

HOT HOT ORANGE BEEF

O odles of this hot, orange-flavored beef is served in Szechuan and Hunan restaurants in Chinatowns everywhere. Five years ago I began trying to recreate it at home but eventually concluded the secret ingredients for this dish were just that! Then I decided to experiment using the same basic ingredients from that other popular Szechuan dish — Kung Pao Chicken — with orange peels and hoisin sauce added. It made sense and it worked! So all you orange beef fans, here it is! This dish is supposed to be wickedly hot: be sure to break up lots of chili pods, adding all of the seeds. Quench the fire with rice and lots of ice-cold beer. For a really hot and spicy dinner, start with Hot and Sour Soup (page 41) served with Pot Stickers (page 18) as an appetizer, then perhaps Mixed Vegetables (page 109). And if you love orange chicken, just substitute ¾ pound boneless thigh (which I prefer) or breast meat, cut into ½-inch cubes, for the beef and use the marinade from page 76.

½ pound flank steak, thinly sliced against the grain

MARINADE
1 large egg white
1 tablespoon soy sauce
1 tablespoon potato or cornstarch
⅛ teaspoon white pepper
½ teaspoon sesame oil

Vegetable oil for stir-frying
2 large garlic cloves, chopped
20 dried red chilies, left whole for mild, 10 broken in half for hot, all broken for very hot
Orange peel from 1 medium orange (slice peel off orange with paring knife into pieces about 1 by 2 inches)

SEASONING LIQUID
Combine in bowl:
1 tablespoon sugar
3 tablespoons hoisin sauce (preferably Koon Chun brand)

(seasoning liquid continued)
1 tablespoon soy sauce
1 tablespoon red wine vinegar
1 tablespoon dry sherry
1 tablespoon chili oil
¼ teaspoon salt
½ teaspoon potato or cornstarch

1 tablespoon sesame oil

• • • • • • • • • • •

1. Combine beef and *marinade* in bowl; marinate 2 hours or up to 24 hours, covered, in refrigerator.

2. Heat wok on high heat. Add 2 tablespoons oil; when hot, add beef and stir-fry for 30 seconds or until medium-rare. Remove to a plate.

3. Return wok to high heat; add 1 tablespoon oil. When hot, add garlic, chilies (including seeds), and orange peel slices. Toss for 30 seconds or until chilies begin to blacken. Return beef to wok, toss for 30 seconds, restir *seasoning liquid,* and pour over beef. Toss for 30 seconds or until glazed by sauce. Drizzle in sesame oil, stir, and transfer to a heated platter.

Serves 2 to 4.

Vegetables being trimmed and arranged in full view of passersby.

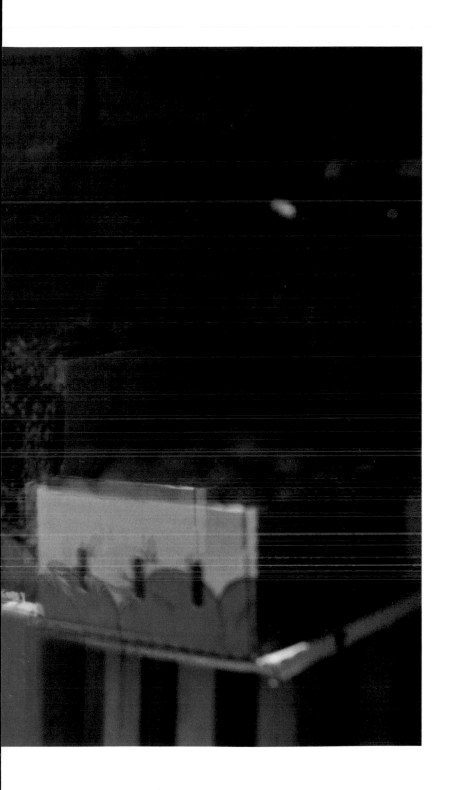

VEGETABLES

HOT AND SPICY WRINKLED BEANS

A spicy Szechuan dish traditionally known as Dry-Fried Green Beans on Chinatown menus because the classical way of cooking the beans was to dry-fry or sauté them very slowly for up to 2 hours in seasonings until shriveled and highly seasoned. Today Chinatown chefs employ a much quicker method, first deep-frying the beans until wrinkled, then stir-frying them with pungent seasonings for just a few seconds. I prefer tender Western string beans for this dish but you may, of course, use Chinese longbeans. Although this dish is excellent hot, it's also delicious served at room temperature.

1 tablespoon chili paste with soy bean
½ teaspoon salt
2 large garlic cloves, chopped
1 tablespoon finely chopped fresh ginger
2 cups oil for frying
¾ pound green beans, ends trimmed, washed, and dried well to prevent spattering

1. Measure chili paste and salt (no need to mix) into a tiny dish; place next to garlic and ginger beside wok.

2. Heat wok on high heat. Add oil; heat to 380°F. Deep-fry beans (standing back in case of spattering) for 1 to 2 minutes or until they are wrinkled and blistered but still bright green.

3. Drain beans, leaving 1 tablespoon oil in wok.

4. Return wok to high heat. Add ginger and garlic; cook for a few seconds. Add chili paste and salt (be sure to scrape out all the seasonings), then return green beans to wok. Stir-fry for 1 minute or until beans are coated and flavored with seasonings.

Serves 2 to 4.

These rustic, deep-fried green beans are for lovers of gutsy, hot and spicy food.

STIR-FRIED SPINACH WITH FERMENTED BEAN CURD

F*ermented bean curd — bottled cubes of bean curd afloat in a hot chili-flecked brine — may not sound or look too appealing to you, yet this deliciously pungent seasoning works wonders on a simple plate of stir-fried spinach. It not only gives a beguiling winey flavor to the greens, it also rounds out and softens the natural harshness of spinach. The first time I was served bean curd "cheese" in Chinatown, it was as a dip mashed with sesame oil to accompany Chinese lamb stew. I had devoured the tiny dish of bean curd dip long before the stew arrived — enjoying every unique-tasting mouthful while trying to figure out what it was — and promptly asked the astonished waiter for more! I particularly like to serve this spinach with Chinese Beef Stew (page 100) but it goes well with any stir-fried meat, fish, or poultry dish.*

2 squares fermented white bean curd
  with chili
2 teaspoons liquid from bean curd
½ teaspoon sugar
3 tablespoons oil for frying
4 large garlic cloves, chopped
10 ounces fresh spinach, with stems
  intact, washed, and dried very well
1 teaspoon dry sherry
Salt

THICKENER
Combine in small bowl:
1 teaspoon potato or cornstarch
2 teaspoons water

1. Mash bean curd with liquid in a small bowl; stir in sugar.

2. Heat wok on high heat. Add oil; when hot, add garlic and cook for a few seconds. Add spinach; continue stir-frying for about 1 minute or until limp. Add bean curd mixture; toss until mixed.

3. Splash in sherry; toss and sprinkle in a little salt.

4. Restir *thickener;* pour into wok and toss to mix. Transfer to heated platter and serve at once.

Serves 2 to 4.

MIXED VEGETABLES

T his glorious vegetable mélange is so compatible with any main dish that it is one of the most requested vegetable platters in Chinatown restaurants. Though I like to experiment with the many different vegetables in the market these days, this is the tried and true combination I always return to. The secret here is to blanch the snow peas and broccoli for only a few seconds — until they turn bright green. Immediately drain them and place in a bowl of ice water to set the brilliant green color, then drain the broccoli very well or there will be too much liquid for the sauce to thicken properly. Now when stir-fried, the broccoli and snow peas will remain bright green, as long as you don't overcook them! The white fungus (silver ears) is an optional ingredient available in Chinatown food shops in clear plastic containers. They look like dried white flowers, have a delicate chewy texture once reconstituted, and no taste of their own, but they absorb the flavors from the sauce.

2 tablespoons vegetable oil

2 large garlic cloves, chopped

1 tablespoon finely chopped fresh ginger

½ small sweet red pepper, seeded and cubed

6 Chinese dried black mushrooms, stems snapped off, caps soaked for 30 minutes in hot water, squeezed dry, and left whole

2 cups broccoli florets (not stems), blanched and drained well

16 snow peas, ends trimmed, and blanched

6 canned baby corn, halved lengthwise

½ cup canned straw mushrooms, sliced in half lengthwise (unless the small variety)

1 dried white fungus, soaked in warm water for 10 minutes, drained well, and cut into 6 to 8 pieces (optional)

SEASONING LIQUID
Combine in bowl:
⅓ cup chicken stock
2 tablespoons oyster sauce
¼ teaspoon salt
2 teaspoons potato or cornstarch

1 tablespoon sesame oil

. . . .

1. Heat wok or large (12-inch) nonstick skillet on high heat. Add oil; when hot, add garlic and ginger. Cook a few seconds; add red pepper.

Add remaining vegetables one at a time, in order listed, tossing for about 15 seconds each before adding next ingredient.

2. Restir *seasoning liquid;* pour into wok and stir until thickened. Drizzle in sesame oil, stir, and remove to a heated platter. Serve immediately.

Serves 4.

STIR-FRIED SNOW PEAS AND CHINESE SAUSAGE

C hinese sausages, a sweet and rich-tasting delicacy, are sold in shrink-wrapped packages or in pairs on strings in Chinatown food shops. There are two kinds. One is made from pork (bright pink in color with white pork fat showing through the casing), the other from duck liver (brownish in color). They must be steamed before stir-frying, but this can be done several hours ahead, the sausages covered with plastic wrap, and refrigerated. Bring them back to room temperature before frying. When combined with sweet, crisp snow peas, they create a vivid and very tasty dish.

3 Chinese (pork) sausages
1 tablespoon vegetable oil
½ pound snow peas, ends trimmed
3 large green onions (white part only), finely shredded
¼ teaspoon salt

1. Place a rack in wok; add water up to bottom edge of rack. Cover wok; bring to a boil.

2. Place sausages on heatproof plate (I use a Pyrex pie plate); place on rack over boiling water. Cover; steam-cook for 10 minutes or until sausage fat is transparent. Remove, allow to cool enough to handle, and slice on the diagonal as thinly as possible.

3. Clean and dry wok. Return to high heat. Add 1 tablespoon oil; when hot, add snow peas, green onions, and salt, adding more oil if necessary. Stir-fry for 30 seconds or until snow peas are bright green. Add sausage; stir-fry another 30 seconds to heat through. Remove to heated serving dish.

Serves 2 to 4.

The perfect accompaniment to any main dish — or serve it with rice as a snack or lunch as the Chinese do.

The humble cabbage is quickly sautéed and enlivened by the piquant presence of chilies and Szechuan peppercorns in a delicate sweet and sour sauce.

SWEET AND SOUR CABBAGE

S imple to prepare, this crisp and crunchy vegetable is delectable and quite stunning in appearance, whether you use all-green or all-red cabbage or a combination of the two (not Chinese cabbage in this case). The secret is not to overcook the cabbage; add the sauce and remove it from the wok as soon as the color heightens.

1 pound green or red cabbage, or a
   combination
3 tablespoons vegetable oil
1 large garlic clove, chopped
2 small dried red chilies, chopped
½ teaspoon Szechuan peppercorns

SEASONING LIQUID
Combine in bowl:
1½ tablespoons sugar
1½ tablespoons soy sauce
1½ tablespoons rice vinegar
1 teaspoon sesame oil
½ teaspoon salt
½ teaspoon potato or cornstarch

1. Cut off base of cabbage; remove tough outer leaves. Quarter cabbage; cut out core. Cut leaves into approximately 1 × 1½- inch pieces. There should be about 4 cups of cabbage.

2. Heat wok on high heat. Add oil; when hot, add garlic, chilies (including seeds), and peppercorns and cook a few seconds. Add cabbage; toss for 1 to 2 minutes or until color brightens from pale green to bright green or deep purple to vivid red. Do not overcook.

3. Stir *seasoning liquid* into wok; toss a few seconds to combine. Immediately remove to a serving dish.

Serves 4 to 6.

EGGPLANT AND RED PEPPER IN FRAGRANT SAUCE

A dazzling dish of Szechuan origin where dark, lustrous eggplant slices contrast with julienned sweet red pepper and green onions in a seductive sauce that is simultaneously sweet, hot, and tart. In Chinatown, it's almost always cooked with ground pork, but I omitted the pork and added red peppers for color and texture. Use either the slender, tender-skinned Oriental eggplants (which don't require pre-salting) or regular eggplant (which must be sliced as directed in recipe, tossed with 1 tablespoon salt, and set aside for at least 30 minutes, then rinsed and dried very well before using). The salting extracts both the moisture and the bitterness, as well as preventing the eggplant from absorbing too much oil. I prefer sautéing this dish in a large (12-inch) nonstick skillet because stir-frying the eggplant in a wok requires too much oil to prevent it from sticking. Even though the skin of regular eggplant is tougher than the Oriental variety, I don't peel them because of their beautiful deep-purple color. But make sure every slice of eggplant is tender before adding remaining ingredients, or it will be undercooked.

3 tablespoons oil
1 pound eggplant, unpeeled, stem removed, cut in half lengthwise, and sliced into ½-inch strips, rather like long thick-cut French fries
1 sweet red pepper, seeded and sliced into ¼-inch strips
2 large garlic cloves, chopped
1 tablespoon finely chopped fresh ginger
1 tablespoon hot bean sauce (preferably Har Har Pickle Food Factory brand)

SEASONING LIQUID
Combine in bowl:
2 tablespoons sugar
1 tablespoon soy sauce
2 tablespoons red wine vinegar

(seasoning liquid continued)
1 teaspoon dry sherry
¼ cup chicken stock

2 whole green onions, chopped
1 tablespoon sesame oil

. . . .

1. Heat large (12-inch) nonstick skillet or wok on high heat. Add oil; when hot, add eggplant. Stir-fry for 5 minutes (reducing heat to medium if necessary) or until every eggplant slice is tender (adding more oil if necessary).

2. Add red pepper, garlic, and ginger; toss another 1 to 2 minutes

or until red pepper is crisp-tender. Stir in hot bean sauce; cook for 30 seconds.

3. Stir in *seasoning liquid*; cook for 30 seconds on high heat, stirring eggplant mixture to absorb liquid. Sprinkle with green onions, then drizzle in sesame oil. Stir and serve at once or at room temperature.

Serves 4.

Everyone raves about this aromatic eggplant dish — even those who claim not to be fans of the vegetable.

GLOSSARY

Chinese cooking requires many ingredients for which there are no substitutes. Most are available only in Chinese or other Asian grocery stores, although some supermarkets are beginning to carry authentic ingredients if they have an "Oriental" food and vegetable section. Many specialty food stores carry Chinese ingredients too.

Towns of every size usually have at least one Chinese restaurant and their proprietors will often sell you ingredients or tell you where to shop for them. Local cooking school staff and caterers may also know where to find ingredients or if you have friends who live near a Chinatown, they can bring or send you what you need. Of course, if you live near a Chinatown or Asian grocery store, you're all set.

Below, I have listed all the special ingredients used in the recipes in this book and where applicable, the specific brands (see photo opposite page) that I have found, through extensive testing, give the best and most authentic Chinatown flavor.

FROM LEFT TO RIGHT, TOP ROW: *white rice vinegar, hoisin sauce, plum sauce, hoisin sauce, golden mushrooms, sliced bamboo shoots, chunked bamboo shoots, oyster sauce, mushroom soy, tea, sesame oil, soy sauce,*

SECOND ROW: *Chinese red vinegar, young corn, white pepper, straw mushrooms, tree ears, red-in-snow, preserved bean curd, spicy salt, fermented black beans, star anise, hot bean sauce, Szechuan preserved vegetable, chili paste with soy bean, Chinese chili sauce, chili oil, dried red chilies, Szechuan peppercorns, hot red chili flakes,*

THIRD ROW: *potato starch, wheat starch, cornstarch, fermented black beans, Chinese dried black mushrooms, rice stick noodles, bean thread noodles, tangerine peel, bean curd sticks, lily buds, rice stick noodles, white fungus,*

BOTTOM ROW: *long grain white rice, sweet rice, sweet red vinegar.*

BABY CORN. Also called "young corn", these are miniature corn cobs, used whole or sliced in stir-fried vegetable and meat dishes. Available canned in Chinese food stores and some supermarkets. Unused portion will keep for up to a week in the refrigerator if left in its brine in a covered glass or plastic container. Recommended brand: Y & Y.

BAMBOO SHOOTS. The edible, ivory-colored shoots of large bamboo plants, appreciated for the crunch and refreshing taste they add to many dishes. Though fresh shoots are sometimes available, the ones I have come across are usually past their prime. I much prefer the canned variety which are available whole, presliced, or in chunks. Winter bamboo shoots are preferred for their exceptional sweetness and crispness. They are available in Chinese grocery stores and some supermarkets. Blanch or rinse them in cold water before using to remove the canned taste. Unused portion will keep for up to a week in the refrigerator if left in its brine in a covered glass or plastic container. (Though all Chinese cookbooks recommend storing the unused portion of canned ingredients in water, I've found that, although ingredients last a little longer, the water leaches out the flavor.) Recommended brands: Ma Ling; Y & Y Strips Bamboo Shoots.

BEAN CURD. Fresh bean curd is made from soy beans that have been soaked, boiled, then pressed, and drained until the curd forms. It is high in protein, low-calorie, and has no cholesterol. Its bland flavor combines well with other foods. Bean curd is sold in plastic containers in the refrigerator section of Chinese grocery stores and some supermarkets. Store in the refrigerator for about 1 week in cold water that is changed daily.

BEAN CURD STICKS. These cream-colored sticks are made from layers of soy bean milk that have been dried. They must be softened by soaking in warm water for 2 hours before using. Rich in flavor, they are usually stewed or braised with meat and vegetables. Sold in cellophane packages in Chinese grocery stores. Avoid packages that look old and that contain a lot of broken bits. The sticks should appear shiny and bright. Discard if they have a strong odor — they should have only a very faint, sweet aroma.

BEAN SPROUTS. These crisp and crunchy shoots are germinated from soy beans (the larger variety) and, more commonly, mung beans. They are sold by weight in Chinese grocery stores and most supermarkets. Choose only white, crisp sprouts. Store them in plastic bags, but only for 3 or 4 days at most. They are very perishable. Also, I never wash them unless they're to be used raw. Do not use canned bean sprouts for the recipes in this book.

BEAN THREAD NOODLES. Also known as cellophane and transparent noodles. These threadlike, dry white noodles are made from mung bean starch. They puff up and turn whiter still when deep-fried, but become soft and gelatinous when soaked. I purchase a brand where several small cellophane packages (about 2 ounces each) are encased in pink plastic webbing. They last indefinitely stored in a dry place at room temperature. Recommended brand: Lungkow Vermicelli (Bean thread).

CHICKEN BREASTS. I have given the weight for chicken breasts with the bone in. If you buy boneless breasts, cut the weight in half to obtain the right amount.

CHICKEN THIGHS. To debone, remove and discard skin. Using a sharp knife, cut around the bone to sever meat and tendons. Begin cutting and scraping the meat down the bone. Continue scraping, while turning the thigh, until meat is separate from the bone in one piece. Lay it out flat and remove any large tendons and membrane. Feel around meat for pieces of bone and remove. Using the top, blunt edge of a cleaver or chef's knife, pound both sides of meat, several times, in various directions to tenderize. (I've recently noticed boned chicken thighs at the supermarket. These are wonderfully convenient — buy several packages, rewrap them into ¾ pound packages, and freeze. Or ask your butcher to debone chicken thighs for you; also specialty poultry butchers in Chinatown sell deboned thigh meat.)

CHICKEN STOCK. It is always preferable to use home-made chicken stock, especially in soup recipes. If you do use canned chicken broth in sauces, use 1 can broth to 2 cans water, or for soups, use 1 can broth to 2 to 3 cans water.

CHILI OIL. A hot oil made from an infusion of red chili peppers, garlic, and vegetable oil. But many brands are quite flavorless and mild, so that it's best to sample a few until you find the one you like. A brand I use is made in Taiwan by Lieh Gee Enterprises, and is labeled simply "Chili Oil" above a drawing of a red chili; or Y&Y brand.

CHILI PASTE WITH SOY BEAN OR GARLIC PASTE WITH CHILI. A hot, reddish-colored condiment made from chilies, garlic, soy beans, and salt. It has its own unique flavor and shouldn't be used as a substitute in recipes calling for hot bean sauce. Keep in the refrigerator where it will last several months — it loses heat after that time. Recommended brand: Lan Chi.

CHINESE CABBAGE. Also called celery cabbage, it has white leaves with light green, crinkly tips. There are two kinds. Use only the short, plump variety — not the long-headed, slim type. Available in Chinese grocery stores and some supermarkets. Store in the refrigerator for up to 2 weeks in a plastic bag.

CHINESE CHILI SAUCE. A hot and spicy sauce made of chili, onion, lemon, sweet potato, and vinegar. I use this sauce as a dip, not as a flavoring in recipes. Once opened, it will keep in the refrigerator for several months. Recommended brand: Koon Yick Wah Kee.

CHINESE CHIVES. Sold in bunches, these have long, flat leaves resembling blades of grass. Delicate in flavor, though stronger than Western chives, they become more pungent as they get older.

CHINESE DRIED BLACK MUSHROOMS. These woodsy, strong flavored mushrooms come in two varieties. The best and most expensive have thick caps with white cracks. These are used mostly in recipes calling for whole caps. The smaller, lower-grade mushrooms are used sliced and as a flavoring. The stems can be snapped off (and saved for flavoring stock or discarded) before soaking the caps in hot water. Sold in cellophane bags and clear plastic boxes in Chinese grocery stores, these mushrooms last indefinitely in a covered container.

CHINESE MUSTARD. Typically made by mixing dry mustard (such as Keen's) and water, for a result that I find rather raw and unpleasant tasting. I make my own version by mixing a couple of tablespoons Dijon mustard with a drizzle of sesame oil to taste (see page 17).

CHINESE SAUSAGE. Two kinds are to be found in Chinese grocery stores: pork, which are pink and have a sweetish flavor, and duck-liver sausage, brown and gamy tasting. Both types are sold in shrink-wrapped packages in the store's refrigerator section. They must be steamed for about 15 minutes before eating. Sausages will keep for weeks in the refrigerator and months in the freezer.

CHINESE TURNIP. Also called daikon radish (Japanese), this white vegetable is shaped like a large sweet potato. It has a crisp, fresh taste and is used mostly in soups and stews. Available at Chinese and Japanese grocery stores.

CORIANDER. Also called Chinese parsley and cilantro. It looks like flat parsley but has an unmistakable, pungent flavor and aroma that I love, but some people dislike. Check with your guests before adding it to a dish or serve it on the side. Generally used as a seasoning or a garnish, coriander can be purchased in Chinese and Asian grocery stores. Choose bunches with bright green, unblemished leaves, preferably with roots attached. Store in refrigerator for 4 to 5 days, with roots in a glass of water, covered with a plastic bag.

CORNSTARCH. The standard thickening agent used in Chinese cooking because it gives a silky translucency to sauces and soups. It also helps to create a crisp coating on deep-fried foods and if part of a marinade, to tenderize and seal in the juices. Cornstarch must be dissolved in cold water or other liquid before using. Since it separates on standing, it must always be restirred before adding to hot sauces or soups. Place a chopstick across the bowl of cornstarch thickener: that way, it's handy for stirring — and a reminder to do so. Also, it never hurts to have an emergency thickener by the stove — 1 tablespoon starch dissolved in 2 tablespoons water — in case a sauce doesn't thicken properly. Don't add all of it at once: drizzle in, a little at a time, to the correct consistency.

DRIED RED CHILIES. These pods are about 2 inches long. They are available whole and when broken or crushed, the seeds produce an even hotter flavor. Sold in supermarkets and Oriental grocery stores, they will keep a long time in a covered container in a cool, dark cupboard.

DRY SHERRY. As a flavoring in sauces and marinades, I use sherry instead of Chinese rice wine, which isn't readily available. Buy a good medium-priced brand because a cheap sherry will impart an unpleasant taste. I've tried several brands and have found that a lightly dry Spanish sherry called EL CID blends well with Chinese ingredients.

EGGPLANT. Chinese eggplants have a pale purple skin and are longer, about 6 to 9 inches, slimmer, and more tender than regular eggplant. They are available at Chinese grocery stores. Look for smooth, unblemished skin. Regular eggplants need presalting and rinsing to remove bitterness, Chinese ones do not.

FERMENTED BEAN CURD. Often labeled Preserved Bean Curd, these are fresh bean curd cubes that have been fermented in Chinese wine. Spicy, winy, and strongly flavored, they are used as a condiment and also as a flavoring for stir-fried greens. Available in Chinese grocery stores in glass jars — you can see the white curds flecked with red chili — this ingredient will keep in the refrigerator almost indefinitely. Recommended brand: Tofu Soy Sauce (Six Fortune).

FERMENTED BLACK BEANS. Also labeled Salted Black Beans, they're made from soy beans that have been fermented (turning them black), then dried, and salted. Pleasantly pungent, they are most often combined with garlic and ginger to complement seafood, poultry, and vegetables. Packaged in plastic bags and cylindrical cardboard boxes, they are sold in Chinese grocery stores. Most cookbooks say to rinse them, but this is not necessary. Store in a covered container in a dark, cool cupboard where they will keep for several years.

FIVE SPICE POWDER. A strongly flavored blend of ground star anise, cinnamon, fennel, cloves, and Szechuan peppercorns that is used as a seasoning. Available in plastic bags in Chinese grocery stores. Transfer to a covered jar and store at room temperature for up to a year. Its flavor fades after that.

FLANK STEAK. This cut of beef is recommended for the stir-fried dishes in this book. It is always tender and flavorful when marinated, then thinly sliced against the grain (i.e., at a right angle to the direction of the fibers) on the diagonal. Flank steak is available at most supermarkets and at meat counters in Chinese grocery stores. Slice a whole flank steak crosswise in 4 fairly equal sections, each will be about 1/2 pound. Wrap each section in two layers of plastic wrap and freeze. When ready to use, partially thaw, then slice on the diagonal. (The slices shouldn't be longer than 2 inches; cut them in half if necessary.) Sirloin or beef tenderloin can be substituted, though the flavor and texture will not be the same.

GARLIC. I use fresh garlic in generous quantities in my cooking. By a "large garlic clove" I mean enough chopped garlic to almost fill a tablespoon. When purchasing garlic, always look for firm, plump cloves.

GINGER. Fresh ginger is an essential ingredient in Chinese cooking. When selecting it look for roots with shiny, smooth, taut skin. Peel before use. Never substitute dry or powdered ginger. Store ginger, wrapped in a paper towel, in a plastic bag in the refrigerator for several weeks. Ginger does not freeze well.

GREEN ONIONS. Also called scallions, they are widely used in Chinese cooking. *To make green onion brushes, trim root ends, cut slits about 2 inches long at both ends; place in ice water to curl ends.*

HOISIN SAUCE. A thick, dark brown sauce made from soy beans, flour, sugar, vinegar, garlic, and chili. It is used as a flavoring, a dip, and a spread. Available in Chinese grocery stores. It will keep for several months in the refrigerator. Recommended brands: Koon Chun (blue and yellow label); Yuet Heung Yuen (orange label).

HOT BEAN SAUCE. Also called chili bean sauce, it is used as a condiment or seasoning. Made from soy beans, chilies, and sesame oil, this sauce is available in Chinese grocery stores. Some brands contain fermented black beans: avoid them for the recipes in this book. Also be aware that there are bean sauces without chilies: check carefully to be sure the word "hot" or "chili" is on the label. Hot bean sauce is not a substitute for chili paste with soy bean: both have their own unique flavor. Recommended brands: Har Har Pickle Food Factory (blue label); Fu Chi (red and white label).

LILY BUDS. Also called golden needles, these dried tiger-lily buds add a delicate floral flavor and textural quality to dishes. They must be softened in cold water before using and the hard ends cut off. Sold in Chinese grocery stores in plastic bags, these should be supple — something you can feel through the package. Avoid hardened ones. Transfer unused lily buds to a covered container and store in a cool, dark cupboard. They will last a few years.

MUSHROOM SOY SAUCE. Similar to black or dark soy sauce but richer in flavor, it can be used in its place. An extract of soy beans, flour, mushrooms, salt, and water, mushroom soy will keep indefinitely. Recommended brand: Pearl River Bridge.

OIL. Any vegetable oil may be used. Peanut and corn oil are very popular and because they have a high smoking point (won't burn at high temperatures), they are excellent for stir-frying and deep-frying. I use canola oil, which is pressed from the rapeseed plant and has the same healthy qualities as olive oil.

OYSTER SAUCE. A richly flavored sauce made from oyster extract, seasonings, and water, used to add flavor to sauces, meats, poultry, and vegetables. The best brands cost a little more, but are worth the extra expense. It keeps indefinitely in the refrigerator. Recommended brand: Lee Kum Kee "Premium".

PLUM SAUCE. A sweet, spicy dipping sauce made from plums, sugar, ginger, chili, and garlic. Avoid domestic brands: the best are made in Hong Kong. Store in refrigerator for 3 to 4 months. Recommended brands: Koon Chun (blue and yellow label) and Yuet Heung Yuen (orange label).

POTATO STARCH. I prefer this "flour" ground from cooked potatoes to cornstarch for thickening sauces and soups (though not as a coating for deep-frying) because it is more gelatinous and gives a subtler, glossier finish to a dish. Potato starch must be dissolved in cold water or other liquid before using. It separates on standing and must be restirred before it is added to soups or sauces. As with cornstarch, I always place a chopstick across the bowl to have it handy for stirring and as a reminder. Also, it never hurts to have an emergency thickener by the stove — 1 tablespoon starch dissolved in 2 tablespoons water — in case a sauce doesn't thicken properly. Don't add all of it at once: drizzle it in, a little at a time, to the correct consistency.

RED-IN-SNOW. A delicious, spinach-like vegetable preserved in salt, this has a crisp, sour taste. It comes in small cans labeled Pickled Cabbage — not red-in-snow. Recommended brand: Ma Ling (yellow label).

RICE. The Chinese most often use long-grain white rice with meals. To make perfect boiled rice, always cook at least 1 1/2 cups raw rice. Rice must first be rinsed under cold water to remove the talc, whether or not the package says it's necessary.

RICE FLOUR NOODLES. Fresh white rice flour noodles are sold in plastic bags in the refrigerator section of Chinese grocery stores. These should appear glossy and oily to guarantee freshness. These noodles last only a day or two, before becoming dry and stale.

RICE STICK NOODLES. Also called rice vermicelli, these wiry, white, thin noodles are made from ground rice. Similar in appearance to bean thread (cellophane) noodles except they don't look as transparent. Sold dried, in tightly folded wads, in 1 pound packages. They need only a brief soaking if used in soups and stir-fries; if deep-frying them, the noodles are separated, but not soaked, and dropped into hot oil for a few seconds until they expand and turn white.

SESAME OIL. A highly fragrant and nutty oil made from roasted sesame seeds. I use a Japanese brand (Kadoya) rather than the Chinese brands which I've often found rancid tasting. Don't use the light-colored cold-pressed sesame oil found in health food stores — it doesn't have enough flavor. Store in refrigerator where it will last several months.

SESAME SEEDS. Both black and white seeds are used as a seasoning and garnish. Sold in cellophane bags in Chinese and Japanese grocery stores.

SNOW PEAS. Flat, green peas with edible pods. Choose young pods which are sweeter and crisper. They require only brief cooking to retain their bright green color and crispness.

SOY SAUCE. Made from fermented soy beans, wheat, salt, and sugar, soy sauce is the most important seasoning in Chinese cooking. It's used for marinating, cooking, and dipping. All the recipes in this book were tested using Chinese soy sauce because Japanese brands (e.g., Kikkoman) impart a slightly sweeter and not totally authentic flavor to Chinese dishes. Soy sauce will last a long time if stored at room temperature. Don't use the synthetic brands available in many supermarkets: they are not suitable for the recipes in this book. Recommended brand: Pearl River Bridge Superior Soy Sauce.

SPICY SALT. Also called Szechuan pepper salt, it's available in plastic containers in Chinese grocery stores. To make your own, dry-fry about 6 tablespoons salt with 4 tablespoons Szechuan peppercorns for about a minute or until fragrant. Remove, cool, and grind in a mortar.

SPRING ROLL SKINS. These thin, delicate, crepe-like wrappers are available in the freezer section of Oriental grocery stores. The best kind are round, not square. They will keep in the freezer for 2 to 3 months if the package is well sealed (they dry out easily) in plastic wrap.

SQUID. To clean, gently pull head and body apart. Cut off the tentacles just in front of the eyes. Squeeze out the beak, located where the tentacles come together (it looks like a small white marble) and discard. Under cold running water, remove all the entrails inside the body sac. Peel off the purple membrane covering the body. Set aside tentacles and cleaned body sac and continue until all are cleaned. Rinse tentacles and follow recipe instructions.

STAR ANISE. A star-shaped seed cluster with a strong licorice flavor. Used in braised and simmered poultry and meat dishes. Sold in cellophane bags in Chinese grocery stores. Avoid packages with dull-looking or many broken clusters. They will keep indefinitely at room temperature stored in a covered container.

STRAW MUSHROOMS. So named because they are grown on beds of rice straw. Straw mushrooms are available both canned (used in the recipes in this book) and dried. Some canned brands contain very small mushrooms which should be left whole. Slice medium-size mushrooms in half lengthwise. Recommended brands: Rowland; Y & Y.

SWEET RICE. Also called glutinous rice, it's a short-grain, opaque rice that becomes sticky and translucent when cooked. Mostly used for sweet and savory stuffings and coatings or in desserts. Sold in 5-pound bags at Chinese grocery stores.

SZECHUAN PEPPERCORNS. Also called flower pepper and wild pepper, these reddish-brown peppercorns aren't really peppers at all, but the dried berries of a shrub. They have a distinctive aroma, but aren't hot. Used in marinades, seasonings, and coatings, they are sold in cellophane packages in Chinese grocery stores. They will keep indefinitely stored in a covered container at room temperature though they lose some fragrance over time.

SZECHUAN PRESERVED VEGETABLE. Canned, chili-encrusted knobs of mustard green — either sliced or diced — add a wonderful salty, hot,

and unusual flavor plus crisp texture to dishes such as Ma Po Pork and Bean Curd and Pork with Szechuan Preserved Vegetable Soup. All Chinese cookbooks suggest rinsing it before use, but I never do. Unused portion will keep indefinitely in the refrigerator if stored in a covered glass jar. Recommended brand: White Rabbit, manufactured by China National Produce Corp.

TANGERINE PEELS, DRIED. Also labeled orange peel, they're used as a flavoring in soups and braised dishes. They are sold in cellophane bags in Chinese grocery stores.

TEA. Tea is appreciated by the Chinese in the same way that fine wines are by the French. Tea is also considered to have many health giving qualities, one being that it's good for the digestion — especially for dissolving oil in the diet. In Chinatown, tea is always brought to the table as soon as the diners are seated and it's drunk throughout the meal. In China, it's either enjoyed before the meal or at the end of it — never during. I buy my tea in a specialty store in Chinatown where there is a large variety to choose from and a good turnover, so that it's always fresh and fragrant. I like to buy several different kinds, only a few ounces at a time. Always store tea in a covered container (metal tea containers are available at tea specialty shops).

The various Chinese teas include: green tea, notable for its fresh taste and aroma. The tea leaves are dried immediately after picking and are not fermented. My favorite green

teas are Shou Mei (Old Man's Eyebrows) and Lung Ching (Dragon Well).

Red tea is called black tea in English. Made from fermented tea leaves, its flavor is strong and aromatic. Ch'i Men (Keemum) is the most famous red tea, with its spicy yet delicate taste. Oolong tea is semi-fermented with a flavor between green and red tea. T'ieh Kuan Yin (Iron Goddess of Mercy) and Shui Hsien (Water Fairy) are popular oolong teas. Scented or flowered teas, such as the well-known jasmine tea, have flower or fruit blossoms mixed with the leaves.

To brew tea, bring fresh water to a full boil: do not under boil or over boil it, or the taste of the tea will be ruined. Rinse teapot with some of the boiling water. Use about 2 tablespoons tea leaves (I put my tea leaves in a tea ball) to a pot that holds about 4 cups water for a light tea, more if you want a stronger tea. Pour boiling water over tea leaves and brew for about 3 minutes (remove tea ball if using) then serve. Two pots of tea, sometimes three, can be brewed using the same tea leaves and many connoisseurs like the second brew best. Don't add sugar, cream, or lemon to Chinese tea.

TREE EARS. Also called wood ears, cloud ears, and black fungus, this dried tree lichen is brown or black in color and used both medicinally and as a vegetable in stir-fried dishes where it adds texture, rather than flavor. Rinse them thoroughly before soaking in hot water where they expand to 3

or 4 times their original size. Available in Chinese grocery stores in cellophane packages. They will keep indefinitely at room temperature in a covered container.

VINEGAR. Chinese vinegars — both red and white — are made from rice. For the recipes in this book, I've used good-quality imported French red wine vinegar in place of Chinese red vinegar and either Chinese (Kong Yen brand) or Japanese (Marukan brand) white rice vinegar. Oriental white rice vinegars are sold at Chinese and Japanese grocery stores.

WATER CHESTNUTS. Once you taste fresh, sweet water chestnuts, which are the bulbs of a water-growing plant, you'll never use the canned variety again. Fresh water chestnuts, which are walnut-size with a brown skin, can be found only at Chinese grocery stores. Squeeze them first when purchasing to avoid any that are soft, and peel them before use. Canned water chestnuts have the same texture but no taste; however, they can be substituted if fresh are unavailable. They are sold in supermarkets and Chinese grocery stores. Rinse them in cold water before using, and store unused portion in its brine in the refrigerator for up to 1-week in a glass or plastic container.

WHEAT STARCH. Wheat flour with the gluten removed. Used to make delicate dumpling wrappers for dim sum such as har gow. Sold in plastic bags and 1-pound boxes in Chinese grocery stores.

WHITE FUNGUS. Also called silver ears, they are a translucent relative of tree ears. They are sold in clear plastic packages in Chinese grocery stores. Soaking makes them transparent, their texture jellylike. Store indefinitely at room temperature.

. . . .

EQUIPMENT

WOK. The world's most versatile cooking utensil, perfectly designed for stir-frying, deep-frying, boiling, braising, and steaming. These round pans with high, smooth, sloping sides ensure that heat spreads rapidly and evenly and prevent food from spilling when stir-frying. They come in several different sizes — 14-inch being the best size for home use — and various metals: aluminum, copper, stainless steel, cast iron, and carbon steel. Since the latter two distribute and retain heat best, they are the only type recommended for stir-frying and deep-frying. For steaming I use a stainless steel wok to preserve the "seasoning" that the process would otherwise boil away on my carbon steel wok. Other woks such as electric and nonstick coated woks are just not suitable for Chinese cooking because they are poor conductors of heat and will never get hot enough for stir-frying.

Woks are available with either metal or wooden handles — I prefer the type that has a single, long wooden handle: you can hold this wok without a pot holder. And although many woks are sold with a metal ring to provide a secure base for steaming and deep-frying, they should be used only for this purpose — preferably on a gas range — never for stir-frying, because the ring holds the wok too far from the heat. If you have an electric stove you must use a flat-bottomed wok that sits directly on the burner in order to obtain the maximum heat required for cooking. (All recipes in this book were tested using a flat-bottomed wok on an electric stove. They're not readily available in Chinese stores, however. I found mine in a non-Chinese kitchenware shop located in Chinatown.) A gas stove is perfect for the classic round-bottomed wok. The flames curl up around the wok providing the even heat that is essential. You will also need a dome-shaped wok lid for steaming and stir-frying.

New woks must be seasoned before use. First, thoroughly wash your new wok several times in hot, soapy water, using a scouring pad to remove greasy factory oil. Rinse well, dry, and place on high heat. Heat wok until hot, then add a few tablespoons of vegetable oil, swirling it carefully around so that the entire inside surface is coated with oil. Toss in a few slices of ginger and whole garlic cloves and cook for a few minutes, then discard them. Repeat 2 or 3 times using new oil and seasonings. Wash wok using a sponge or wok brush (a stiff wooden brush for cleaning woks is available in Chinese stores): you must never again use a scouring pad. The wok will darken with continued use (deep-frying will speed up the darkening process), and so it should: this will prevent food from sticking. So don't try to scrub away the "seasoning" — a blackened wok is one sign of a good Chinese cook!

WOK SPATULA OR WOODEN SPATULA. Used to stir-fry and toss ingredients in a wok. The metal, long-handled spatula is designed specifically for using with a wok and is available in Chinese shops. I find the noise of metal scraping against metal irritating, so I prefer the standard wooden spatulas that are available in most kitchenware shops.

WIRE-MESH STRAINER. Chinese bamboo-handled strainers come in various sizes. They are the best choice for lowering food into hot oil or boiling water and removing it when cooked. They make it easy to hold the food over the wok so that excess oil or water will drain off.

DEEP-FRY THERMOMETER. I find a thermometer essential to ensure the correct temperature for deep-frying, then to be sure that it's maintained. You need one that registers up to 400° F — Taylor manufactures an excellent thermometer that is available in restaurant supply stores and some kitchenware shops.

CLEAVERS. I have several cleavers in varying weights: heavy for chopping through bones, medium and light weights for general use. I actually prefer my light, slicing cleaver to a chef's knife, and use it for most types of cutting, chopping, dicing, and slicing. Carbon steel blades are recommended, although they require extra care, e.g., washing and drying them immediately after use to prevent rust. They're also much easier to keep razor sharp. Cleavers are versatile tools: as well as the cutting functions, the flat side of the blade is used for crushing garlic and ginger, for scraping up and transporting chopped ingredients from board to wok or preparation tray, and the blunt top edge to pound and tenderize meat. Cleavers are available in Chinese and some other kitchenware shops.

STEAMERS. There are two types of steamers: metal and bamboo, both of which fit inside the wok over boiling water. Two or three baskets can be stacked on top of each other and food to be cooked is placed either directly in the steamer or on a heatproof dish and then in the steamer. Although I have several bamboo steamers of varying sizes, often I simply put a round metal rack — the kind used for cooling cakes — in the wok over boiling water, then place the food in a heatproof dish on it, and cover with a wok lid.

CHOPSTICKS. Chopsticks are used not only as eating utensils but also as cooking tools. They are used for mixing, beating, testing for doneness, stirring, turning, removing food from deep-frying oil, and picking up ingredients to transfer them during preparation. Chopsticks may be made of bamboo and other woods, of plastic or ivory.

For cooking, unlacquered bamboo or other wooden ones are best: they can withstand high temperatures and don't conduct heat. For eating, bamboo, wooden, and plastic are easiest to use — highly polished and lacquered bamboo chopsticks are very slippery, making it difficult for the novice — or anyone else — to pick up food. It's a good idea to keep at least a dozen plain wooden or bamboo chopsticks in a container by the stove for mixing purposes. It's also fun to collect various kinds and colors of chopsticks for table settings.

TABLEWARE. The basic place setting for an informal Chinese meal consists of a pair of chopsticks, a soup bowl and soup spoon, a rice bowl, and a small plate for bones. A formal setting may include chopstick rests and individual plates instead of rice bowls. For authenticity, I think porcelain soup spoons are essential, as are chopsticks, and I also like to use Chinese serving platters: they are much smaller (only 9 to 10 inches long) than Western platters which are too large for most typical servings. If you don't want to purchase small platters, standard dinner plates are an excellent substitute. When serving Chinese meals, I sometimes like to break with tradition, too, and often mix Italian dinnerware with Chinese — or even Japanese — things.

ELECTRIC RICE COOKER. I cook a lot of rice and find an automatic rice cooker indispensable. Besides supplementing the stove, it's wonderfully foolproof. The washed rice is placed in the container with water added to about 1 inch above its surface, then it's covered and turned on. That's all there is to it! No need to watch the pot — it shuts off automatically when done and keeps the rice warm until serving time. Rice cookers are available in Chinatown shops.

NONSTICK SKILLET. Although a heavy cast-iron or carbon steel wok is the best utensil for stir-frying, a large, high-sided, 12-inch skillet with a nonstick coating is an excellent substitute. (It must be heavy and of high quality — not a flimsy pan — the kind that are available only at restaurant supply stores and better kitchenware shops; one recommended brand name is Wear-Ever, distributed by Mirro/Foley Company.) If I'm stir-frying more than one dish at a time on my electric stove, I place my wok on one burner and the skillet on another because there just isn't room for two flat-bottomed woks. Also, less vegetable oil is needed to stir-fry ingredients in a nonstick pan, so reduce oil accordingly.

TRAYS. As you are chopping and mixing ingredients for a Chinese dish — or dishes — the seasonings, meats, and vegetables should be placed in separate piles along with bowls of premixed liquid seasoning and cornstarch mixture on a preparation tray that is set beside the wok. I use plastic trays (about 13 by 17 inches) that are available at Ikea and restaurant supply stores.

BOWLS. Small- and medium-size stainless steel bowls are useful for everything from mixing thickener to marinating ingredients.

. . . .

C O O K I N G

M E T H O D S

STIR-FRYING. The most popular method of Chinese cooking and the most familiar to North Americans, since 90 per cent of the dishes ordered in Chinese restaurants are stir-fried. Ingredients for stir-frying are cut into uniform, bite-size pieces, quickly and continuously tossed in a wok with a spatula over high heat, sauced, and completed in only a few minutes. It is imperative to heat the wok before adding oil so as to prevent ingredients from sticking, and then to maintain high heat during cooking — unless a recipe specifies otherwise. Everything must be prepared and ready for cooking before you begin. Once you've begun stir-frying there is no time to cut and chop or to run around looking for a missing ingredient. And once the oil is added to the preheated wok, the seasonings (garlic and ginger) must be added immediately, before the oil overheats, then the ingredients must be added before the seasonings burn — all this is happening in a matter of seconds over intense heat! *Never* double recipes: too many ingredients will overwhelm the wok's capacity, stewing the food instead of frying it.

DEEP-FRYING. An important technique in Chinese cooking, deep-frying can be both appetizing and healthy as long as certain rules are carefully followed. To begin with, any flavorless vegetable oil, e.g., canola oil, can be used for frying, though most Chinese chefs prefer peanut oil or corn oil because they can be heated to high temperatures without burning.

Though it's healthier to use fresh oil each time, many people like to economize by reusing cooked oil. If doing so, strain cooled oil through a few layers of paper towels into a clean container with a lid and refrigerate. Before using, add half fresh oil to the cooked oil (each time it's reused), and discard oil once it darkens or develops a strong, cooked odor: it is very unhealthy and highly unappetizing at this point. Never stint on the amount of oil and always deep-fry at the temperature specified in the recipe, maintaining the heat throughout cooking. If the oil is not hot enough, the food absorbs it, becoming greasy and soggy. If the oil is too hot, the food sometimes literally explodes — which is quite dangerous — or it will burn on the outside, but remain uncooked inside. Use a deep-frying thermometer to check the temperature of the oil at all times unless you are expert at judging oil temperature.

I recommend either a flat-bottomed wok or heavy pan for deep-frying, but if you choose to use a round-bottomed wok, be sure to use the wok ring to hold it steady. Food should be as dry as possible and properly coated in batter or cornstarch: never add water to hot oil or it will sputter dangerously. Use chopsticks, tongs, or a wire mesh strainer to lower food gently — never drop it — into the oil. As a precaution, stand back as you're adding food in case of spattering. Do not overload the oil with food: this reduces the temperature, resulting in soggy, greasy food (if oil drops below 350° F for longer than a few seconds, remove food, bring oil back to correct temperature, and return a few pieces at a time). Use chopsticks or tongs along with a wire-mesh strainer or slotted spoon to move and turn the food around and prevent pieces from sticking together. Use the same strainer or spoon to remove food from oil — holding a few pieces at a time over the wok to allow excess oil to drain off before draining on paper towels. Lastly and most importantly, *never* leave a wok full of hot oil unattended — even for a moment. Hot oil is flammable.

STEAMING. Steaming is not only one of the healthiest methods of cooking since the nutrients aren't boiled away, it is also one of the easiest and least demanding. And compared to dishes cooked by other methods, steamed dishes are more subtle in taste, with freshness of ingredients intensified at the same time. Steaming by wet heat is the usual method — the ingredients are placed on a heatproof dish or directly in the steamer set on a rack or tier of a bamboo or aluminum steamer, then placed over boiling water in a wok, and covered. The intense steam from the boiling water circulates and cooks the food. The Chinese have recipes for steaming virtually every type of food: dim sum, breads and buns, poultry, pork, meat, fish, seafood, and vegetables. I use a rack placed in a stainless steel wok for steaming but you can also use a rack in a roasting pan with a lid. Always steam over high heat, keeping an eye on the water level if steaming several batches, and replenishing boiling water if necessary.

.   .   .   .

CUTTING AND PREPARATION TECHNIQUES

SLICING. Cutting into straight, vertical or diagonal slices about 1/8 inch thick and about 1 1/2 inches square. Straight slicing is for ingredients such as ginger or mushrooms and diagonal for vegetables and meats such as celery, carrots, and flank steak. (See Glossary for instructions for slicing a whole flank steak.) Meat or poultry is always easier to slice if it's partially frozen.

MATCHSTICK-SIZE SHREDS. Meat or vegetables are first sliced as described above, then a few pieces are stacked on top of each other and cut into julienne strips.

DICING. Ingredients are first sliced, then stacked on top of each other, sliced into strips, then cut across the length into small pieces.

CHOPPING. Cutting into irregular dice.

CUBING. Cutting into 3/4- to 1-inch cubes.

ROLL CUTTING. Used mainly for carrots and Chinese turnip. Slice off one end at a 45-degree angle. Roll vegetable a quarter turn and slice again to cut another triangular-shaped cube. Continue turning a quarter turn for each cut.

SMASHING. Pounding and lightly flattening ingredients such as garlic or ginger with the flat side of a cleaver or large knife.

MARINATING. Used to season ingredients, and also to tenderize (usually by adding liquid or egg white and cornstarch: they give the food a tender, velvety texture when cooked). The cornstarch helps both to tenderize and seal in the juices during cooking. After ingredients are sliced and placed in the bowl with the marinade, use chopsticks to stir in one direction until marinade is absorbed. Many ingredients need only a short marination, about 30 minutes, although most are improved if left a minimum of 2 hours or even overnight in the refrigerator.

DEVEINING SHRIMPS. Peel shrimps, then make a small incision along the center of the back. Remove the dark vein and discard.

INDEX

Numbers in italic refer to photographs.

. . . .

A sliced orange: the perfect, refreshing finish to a Chinese meal.